THE BIG BOOK OF OF SECRET HIDING PLACES

By Jack Luger

Breakout Productions
Port Townsend, Washington

The Big Book Of Secret Hiding Places

© 1987 by Loompanics Unlimited
© 1999 by Breakout Productions

Published by:
Breakout Productions, Inc.
PO Box 1643
Port Townsend, WA 98368

ISBN 1-893626-09-1
Library of Congress Card Catalog 99-60236

TABLE OF CONTENTS

INTRODUCTION

This book will give you a flying start at the art and science of purposeful concealment. These chapters will show you how to hide both large and small objects in both temporary and permanent locations.

This isn't just another "How To Construct Secret Hiding Places" book. It's not a text on carpentry or excavation. This book covers the dynamics of successful concealment to an extent that no other book in this field has yet done. Note especially the chapters on concealing weapons and on unconventional methods of getting your material "lost" for a period of time.

Some may think that hiding things is necessarily illicit, and that anyone with a clear conscience has literally "nothing to hide." This is untrue, as we can see by examining a few instances.

Let's look at a few people with good reasons to construct hiding places. The first will be someone worried about burglary. He knows that no amount of locks, alarms, and police protection guarantees against intruders ripping off his valuables, such as a coin collection.

Another example is a police officer with young children. He needs to keep his weapons and ammunition away from their small hands, as they're yet too young to understand safe gun handling and an admonition of "Don't touch!" leaves too much to chance.

Even without children, a police officer has to worry about other dangers. His home is as vulnerable to burglary as any civilian's. It can be very embarrassing when an intruder makes off with his service revolver when he's off-duty and away from home. Recently, one young patrolman was ripped off in exactly this way. What made it worse is that his father is the local Chief of Police!

Closely related to this situation is that of a hunter and sportsman who keeps an array of firearms in the house. He knows that no warnings to children below a certain age will be effective, and that even when his children are old enough to understand safe gun handling, those of visitors may not be. It's simpler all around to keep firearms safely out of sight and out of reach.

Another individual keeps a lot of valuables around because he doesn't trust banks. He knows that banks can fail, in which case his assets may or may not be protected by the government. In any event, he knows that if his bank fails, he'll have a long wait for his assets, at best. He needs a place for his bills.

A dealer in valuables, such as stamps, coins, or precious stones may use a safe and an alarm system to protect the bulk of his goods, but may want to handle especially valuable items in a special way, by concealing them.

Yet another earns undeclared income in the underground economy. He has assets to hide not only from thieves but from the government. He knows that safe-deposit boxes are not as safe as they seem, and that even a private vault means entrusting valuables to others' honesty and convenience. He decides that he wants his assets totally under his control.

Carrying concealed weapons is a special topic within the broader one. It's worth close study because, while keeping material concealed is not illegal, carrying a weapon concealed is, in some jurisdictions.

Criminals, of course, tend to carry concealed weapons, which is what gave rise to the laws pertaining to them. What the law doesn't officially acknowledge is that in most instances a concealed weapon is on the person of an otherwise law-abiding citizen who carries it as a defense against crime.

You don't need to see the film *Death Wish* or the TV production *Outrage* to understand that street crime is widespread in this country. You need only read the daily newspaper or watch the TV news to see that, not only are many of our citizens victims of crime, but that the police don't do much to defend them. The first, and usually the only, line of defense is the armed citizen.

Granted it's illegal, and if you live in the hostile environment of New York City, it's *verrry* illegal. It comes down to the basic question: "Would you rather be tried by twelve or carried by six?"

Don't make the mistake of being too open about your hiding places. Some people brag about them, and openly display them to friends and acquaintances. Those who carry weapons, especially, are tempted to show them off. This breaks their low profile and can lead to complications. If you have a need for a hiding place, you may already have a need to be discreet. Such would be the case if you're part of the underground economy. Continue this practice and you'll save yourself needless problems.

A BIT OF HISTORY

Although people have been hiding their possessions and themselves at various times since before the dawn of written history, there is very little written on the subject. The cultural explosion of the Twentieth Century has brought about the greatest volume of literature on hiding and hiding places, and yet there are very few books as such. Previously, there was almost nothing.

Part of the reason is that most people in the world were illiterate before our time. Another is secrecy. Many of these techniques and places for hiding things and people were truly deep and dark secrets, at least in the inventors' minds.

The residue of history is legend and myth. We find this in Britain, where there are many legends about secret tunnels, and most of these legends have no factual basis.[1] People apparently need to believe in romanticized versions of history, and many "secret tunnels" found were actually drains in the old days. With all that, there are some genuine hiding places still existing, and they date from the days of the Catholic persecution in Britain.[2]

The reason for the hidey holes was clear and crisp. Catholic priests risked execution if caught. These were the hearty Elizabethan days of the rack in the Tower of London. Sometimes the victims took days to die under torture.

In Warwickshire, Baddesley Clinton is a stone mansion with three wings surrounding a courtyard. Around it is a moat. In the back wing is a full length tunnel.[3] One exit from it is on the moat, and allegedly there was a plank to bridge the moat for a quick escape. This is unlikely, given the forty foot length required, but the tunnel did serve as a hiding place. There was a secret entrance built into a window seat in what was allegedly the priest's room.

In Aston Hall, in Birmingham, there is a very well preserved hiding place under a stair. A chair is mounted against a wall, and this chair swings aside to reveal a room that measures six by ten feet.[4]

A place with the guttural sounding name of Thrumpton Hall, Nottinghamshire, has a combination secret staircase and cellar room, with the entrance to the underground room hidden in the staircase. The cellar room measured two and one half feet wide by six feet long. It was a tight fit.[5]

In Burghwallis Hall, Yorkshire, there's a false staircase head accessible only from the attic. Over a doorway is a secret trap door which leads onto a crawlway in the attic. Retracing the path along about thirty feet brings the fugitive to a six foot square hiding place at the top of the stairs.[6]

In Hardwick Hall is a false chimney section in the attic. A section is butted onto the real chimney, with a door made of wood covered with plaster and painted to look like a chimney's brickwork.[7]

These are the homes of the nobility and of the gentry. No doubt, working class people and peasants had their secret places too, although not to hide the clergy. Probably they hid their few coins against the tax collector. As money was usually made of a "noble metal," it would stand up to burial for years without corroding.

Across the English Channel, many miles inland and many years later, there was a prisoner-of-war camp at Colditz Castle, now in East Germany. During World War II, the hard-core, "incorrigible" Allied POWS were incarcerated here by the Germans. Security was as total as German ingenuity could devise, and the staff outnumbered the prisoners. Still, there were escapes.

Possibly the most imaginative escape project involved a secret room about forty feet long built into one of the attics of Colditz Castle. This refuge served as a secret workshop for building a glider with a wingspan of thirty three feet, designed to carry two men from a launching pad on the castle roof.

The room itself was closed off from the rest of the attic by a frame wall, covered with canvas and with a superficial layer of plaster to simulate the stone walls of the castle. The plaster was improvised from the debris of another project, a tunnel out of the castle. Materials for the construction of the wall's framework and the glider itself came from the prisoners' theater floorboards. Mattress covers supplied the fabric for the wings and fuselage.[8]

The plan was to launch the glider from the roof, along a catapult rail made of wooden trestles. The wood came from the bunks. The motive power for the launch was to be a bathtub filled with concrete that the prisoners would drop through holes in the floors, for a total drop of three stories. A rope from the bathtub would be attached to the glider, and tow it up to flying speed.

The glider never flew. By the time it was finished, it was the end of the war, and escape was pointless. The glider probably still lies in the attic, deep behind the Iron Curtain.

Other countries no doubt have their secret histories of hiding places, and perhaps some written traces of fact and legend can be found in foreign libraries. However, these are surely outnumbered by the hiding places of modern day America!

NOTES

1. *Secret Hiding Places,* Granville Squiers, (Detroit, Tower Books, 1971) p.14.

2. *Ibid.,* p. 20.

3. *Ibid.,* p. 31.

4. *Ibid.,* p. 43. Photo of this arrangement is on plate facing page 48.

5. *Ibid.,* pp. 81-83.

6. *Ibid.,* pp. 115-117.

7. *Ibid.,* pp. 133-135.

8. *Colditz, The Great Escape,* Ron Baybutt, (New York, Little, Brown & Company, 1982) pp. 124-125.

THE OTHER SIDE OF THE HILL:
PART I — THE SEARCHERS

To develop your ability to hide things, you should understand the mentality and the methods used by those who will be trying to find your hidden material. The insight you gain from examining your potential adversaries will help you understand your task better.

Let's start by laying out one fundamental fact. The success of your effort at hiding something will depend mostly on who's searching, not the ingenuity of your idea or the quality of your workmanship. You might find this hard to believe, but let's examine a few possible situations to see how this works.

(1) You're female, driving alone in your car, carrying about an ounce of cocaine. You come to a roadblock, with heavily-armed sheriff's deputies and state troopers searching every car going in your direction. Troopers on each side of the road are scanning the stopped cars, rifles and shotguns at port arms. As you pull up to the front of the line, a trooper approaches your car from each side, peering into the back seat and into the well in front of the front seat. One trooper asks you to get out and open your trunk, while the other covers him. He explains to you that they're looking for an escaped convict, who is armed, dangerous, and has a history of kidnapping people to help him escape.

In this situation, they're just looking for a human body, and inspecting any space large enough to hide one. You could smuggle a pound of hash or even a machine-gun and not have the police bother trying to find it.

(2) You're a warehouse owner, and one fine morning the police arrive with a search warrant. Their affidavit, based on "information received," states that you may be holding some stolen television sets. They proceed to search your premises. Actually, you're a bookie on the side, and your betting slips are in a drawer of your desk, but the police don't even look inside.

(3) You're a spy, and one night you're awakened by the counter-espionage police who break into your home, arrest you, and start taking the place apart. Several hours later, in the interrogation room, an officer of the counter-espionage police enters and tells you that they've found your miniature camera, invisible ink, and your radio transmitter. Although you'd taken every precaution to hide these well, you know that he's telling the truth and start calculating if you can escape the firing squad by confessing and revealing the identities of your contacts.

From this, we see that there are different levels of search effort, and different agencies performing searches for contraband and stolen goods. Their effort and expertise will vary with the situation, and in most instances, a slight effort at avoiding suspicion will save you embarrassment and arrest. In other situations, nothing you can do will save you, because if there's anything to be found, the officers will find it.

Let's look in detail at the types of searchers we may encounter, and the intensity of the searches they may conduct. These vary widely, from routine and cursory searches to very intense efforts by teams of specialists.

STORE AND PLANT SECURITY

This can vary from slight to intense, and is usually not much of a threat. Store security is usually directed against shoplifters, and consists mainly of covert surveillance by plainclothes officers and TV cameras. Customers are not routinely searched upon exit. Only when an officer has witnessed a theft can he make an arrest and conduct a search.

Plant security is another matter. Industrial plants vary widely in type and in security measures taken. Some have a watchman at the gate, to ensure that an employee doesn't walk out with half the plant stuffed into his lunch box or his pockets. Others are more serious.

Those doing military contract work will tend to have armed guards and examination of all briefcases and packages taken in or out of the plant. These searches may be regular or spot searches. There will also be high security areas within the plant, with restricted access and special rules. Employees and visitors may be required to empty their pockets before entering or when leaving, or even to strip down and change clothing altogether.

Nuclear plants are generally very secure, with a lot of effort directed at controlling who and what comes in. Visitors may be asked to submit to strip searches. This skirts the law somewhat. An individual doesn't have to submit to search, but the plant authorities don't have to let him in, either. Likewise, employees may feel affronted at being searched, but they don't have to work there, either.

It can get pretty grim in certain other countries. In South Africa, for example, workers in diamond mines go through rigorous searches before being allowed to leave. They work in the mines, and are kept in fenced-in compounds, until the period of leave, when they may leave the premises to visit the outside world. Before being allowed to leave, the departing workers are kept in a quarantine area, where they're obliged to take a laxative upon entry. The quarantine lasts long enough for the laxative to take effect, and they're closely watched to make sure that they're not smuggling any diamonds out in their bowels. They are also X-rayed to seek out diamonds secreted in other parts of the body. A strip search is the last step before leaving. This sort of close examination is alien to most Americans, but in other countries, especially if there's a discriminated against caste, it's normal.

AIRPORT SECURITY

With the skyjackings and attacks at airports during the last couple of decades, this is going to become tighter. Today, visitors to the concourse areas of air terminals have to pass through electronic gates and X-ray search of their carry-on luggage. This is aimed mainly at the smuggling of weapons on board aircraft. It has nothing to do with, and does not usually detect, narcotics or other contraband.

There are two types of luggage: carry-on and check-in. The check-in luggage is not accessible in flight, and is not usually examined. Carry-on is stowed under the seat or in overhead racks and bins. Airport security usually scrutinizes this type closely.

How effective is this sort of search in its intended role? It varies widely from one airport to another. In one instance, the author was able, with the cooperation of security guards, to pass a briefcase containing glass fiber daggers under the X-ray to determine whether or not they would show. They did not. In another instance, a security officer at the same airport was able to pass through the electronic gate without triggering the alarm, although he had his Government Model auto pistol under his coat.[1]

THE SPECIAL CASE OF EL AL

El Al, the Israeli airline, has had a special security problem, because of the intense effort directed against it. It has, consequently, special security measures to forestall certain types of attacks, although these measures simply don't work well.

All luggage is searched. This is to forestall the smuggling of both weapons and bombs. El Al takes a special precaution with check-in luggage. All passengers boarding are checked off a list, and if any passenger doesn't make the flight, his luggage is taken off and examined, as this "phantom passenger" technique is a useful way of getting a bomb aboard an airliner. Because some attackers are willing to give up their lives to destroy an El Al airliner, all check-in luggage is searched as carefully as carry-on baggage.

All passengers are physically searched. Travelers on El Al had better arrive early, because airline security officers have booths where they search passengers for weapons. The search can involve stripping to the skin, if the security officer feels that it's necessary.

Where El Al can arrange it, its aircraft get a security escort along the taxiways of the airport, to forestall a surprise ground attack. An armored car or truckload of soldiers escorts it to the end of the runway.

Armed guards travel on each El Al flight. These are supposed to cope with any in-flight attempts to skyjack the aircraft. There's no official confirmation, of course, but rumor has it that the pilots have orders not to divert to an unfriendly country, even if threatened with death. Another rumor is that pilots are ordered to crash the plane rather than divert the flight. Whether they would do this in practice is speculative, as no recent in-flight diversion has occurred. Instead, attacks have taken other forms.

These efforts still don't stop attacks, as the recent experiences in Europe have pointed up. The terminals are still vulnerable. El Al ticket offices, usually located on main boulevards in major cities, are open to both bombing and attacks by gunfire. Slow flying El Al airliners are vulnerable within several miles of the runway, beyond the reach of escort and still low enough to be within reach of ground fire on the approach and take off.

A form of in-flight attack against which there is no defense is the identification and overpowering of the armed guards by unarmed attackers. "Birddogs" flying an El Al route can quickly determine who the guards are, because they shuttle back and forth and some may board the aircraft ahead of the passengers. Once identified, they are vulnerable because attackers can seat themselves close enough to take them by surprise.

CUSTOMS

The severity of customs inspection varies from country to country, with some watching their entering traffic more closely than others. We often find a double standard in customs inspection. Tourists are usually passed through with minimal delay, because the host country doesn't want to discourage visitors. Even visitors to the Soviet Union report that they were treated courteously by Soviet Customs agents. Citizens returning from abroad, on the other hand, get much closer inspection. Customs officials, instead of casually chalking their initials upon their luggage, have them open every case.

In some countries, customs officials will ask each traveler if he has "anything to declare." Sometimes this is a routine question, but at other times, the officer is required to ask it two or three times. This is a requirement of the law, so that a traveler can't claim that he misunderstood or did not hear the question.

POLICE SEARCHES

There are two types: warrantless searches and searches in execution of a warrant. Warrantless searches may be incidental to an arrest, when the arresting officer is permitted to search the prisoner for weapons and evidence. This type of search can be superficial or quite thorough, depending on the situation and the officer.

The "pat down" is going out of style. It was never very effective in disclosing weapons or other contraband, and many police officers now use a caressing motion, sliding the hand along the body to reveal suspicious bulges.

Some locales have "stop and frisk" laws. These permit a police officer to search a suspect superficially while he detains him for a few minutes to verify his identity. The search may disclose weapons or contraband.

When a police officer executes an arrest warrant, this implies the right to search the person and the area under his immediate control. The search of the immediate area holds whether the arrest is a warrant arrest or an impromptu one, because the offender's been caught in the act.

A search warrant is somewhat different, and does not necessarily imply an arrest. For a search warrant, the officer has to present an affidavit to a court detailing his reasons for believing that a search of certain premises will be productive. He may cite evidence in the affidavit, or he may cite an informer who "has been reliable in the past."[2]

In the affidavit, the officer must describe generally what he expects to find. His search authorization is then limited to those items, or that category. For example, if the warrant is for narcotics, and the officer also finds illegal weapons, he can't take them in evidence, because they're "excluded." This rule stems from court decisions designed to prevent abuses such as "fishing expeditions" by police.

No police officer or department will admit this, but it's often expedient to lay the groundwork for a search warrant by an illegal and surreptitious entry before writing the affidavit. The officer conducts a clandestine search for his evidence. He cites it on his affidavit, and when he returns openly to execute the warrant thus obtained, he knows what he's seeking and exactly where to find it. This is the procedure that was called a "black bag job" in FBI slang.

COUNTER-ESPIONAGE POLICE

These are the "tough cookies," the ones hardest to fool and sidetrack. Generally, counter-espionage agents are the best educated, the best paid, and the best motivated. Usually, they can't be bought off or corrupted in any way.

Because espionage paraphernalia can be hidden anywhere, in almost anything, these people will have warrants that permit the most exhaustive searches. The search can easily last for several days, and may disclose one-time code pads, invisible ink, microfilms and microfilming equipment, microdots, and other documents and equipment. Material may be hidden in secret compartments in tables, under floorboards, in hidden rooms, toothpaste tubes, and even in hollowed out coins.

From all of this we can see that almost all depends on the motivation, skill, and diligence of the searchers. With the proper outlook, and the proper tools, they can find practically anything. Let's look at some of their tools next.

NOTES

1. Personal acquaintance of the author's.

2. A form of language which usually satisfies legal requirements. Because police keep the identities of their informers secret, and are supported by the law in doing so, they often invent their informers.

THE OTHER SIDE OF THE HILL:
PART II — THE TOOLS AND TECHNIQUES

The most powerful tool the searcher has is his mind, just as the most powerful weapon you have is yours. Using common sense will often make up for a lack of tools, or inadequate equipment.

The searcher's hands are next. Much searching consists of simply opening and moving things. In body searches, sliding the hands along the contours of the body and feeling for bulges that don't belong is a vital technique. Tactile sense is therefore critical to searching.

Eyeballing the area often helps find contraband. The searcher looks for things that are out of place, tool marks, leaks of fluids, fresh paint, fresh dirt, signs of tampering, and at the same time he scans the suspect closely. Often, a customs officer or policeman will strive to make eye contact with the suspect, going so far as to say, "Look at me when I'm talking to you!" This is in search of the "recognition response reaction." The theory is that the guilty suspect will be more apprehensive than the innocent person, and will crack under the strain of maintaining eye contact, and may try to escape. To the guilty party, eye contact equals an accusing look, according to this theory. It should be obvious that this will work only in the case of a suspect with a very limited mentality.

One technique of searching is measurement, either by eye or by tape measure, seeking hidden spaces and secret compartments. A false bottom in a suitcase can be obvious to a searcher who compares the exterior and interior dimensions, and allows for the thickness of the material. A hidden room in a house will soon come to light when a searcher draws a quick floor plan and includes dimensions.

The ears are also helpful in searching, especially for large spaces. Secret rooms may reveal hollow sounds where the seeker would expect a dull "thud." Sounding for empty spaces is a valuable technique.

Another technique is disassembly. We all know that there are many empty spaces in manufactured objects, and a logical step is to take them apart. Disassembly can be simple, as in opening a portable radio to see if the battery compartment contains batteries or something else. It can be more complicated and even require tools.

A kit of tools is essential for any competent search, especially when there are small objects involved. It may be necessary to unscrew every light switch plate in a house, and to remove every piece of molding, in a search for drugs. Taking the plumbing system apart may disclose contraband, and every appliance is a potential hiding place.

SPECIAL INSTRUMENTS

A basic instrument is a search mirror. This can be a small inspection mirror, which looks something like a dentist's mirror, or it can be much larger, with a pole several feet long, for looking under motor vehicles.

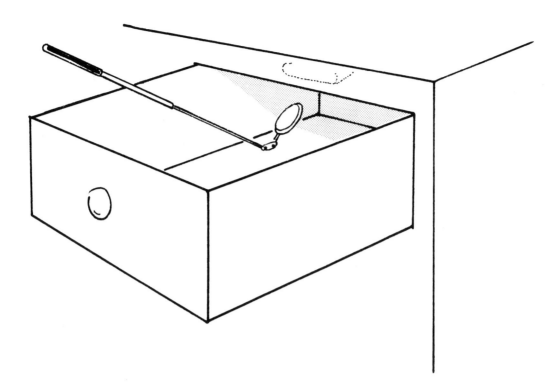

Inspection mirrors

Metal detectors are in common use at airports, of course, but the small portable kinds have other uses. A hand held detector serves for a surreptitious "frisk" for a weapon. A member of a VIP's bodyguard team can pass through a crowd quickly frisking people without touching them.

Airport metal detectors can turn up very small objects, but this can be a severe handicap. The sensitivity is adjustable, and most operators have the sensitivity control set low, to avoid an excessive number of false alarms. Too many false alarms over pens and watchbands can have the security officers ordering people to return to the other side of the gate and empty their pockets out before passing through once more. This can hold up traffic severely, especially at a busy airport. The security officers, who are usually poorly paid "rent-a-cops," don't want the hassle of angry passengers, and they find it easiest to reset the sensitivity control and let things slide.

Metal detectors can find very small bits of metal, some as small as needles or paperclips. Most will pick up non-ferrous metals, such as the brass, lead, and nickel used in ammunition.

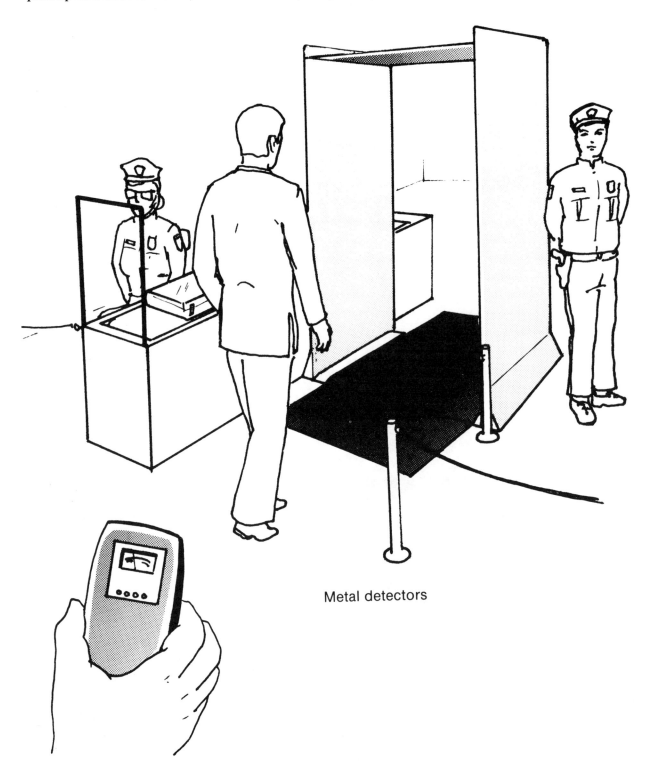

Metal detectors

Both distance and mass affect metal detectors. To pick up a small object, the device has to be very close. A larger object can escape detection at a distance. In practical terms, weapons can evade metal detectors if deeply buried. To find the suitable depth, it's necessary to use trial and error with the metal detectors used in your area. Keep in mind that police and troops seeking buried objects usually use mine detectors, which are somewhat more powerful.

X-ray apparatus is now very portable, and many police and security agencies use it to detect both weapons and bombs. The fixed installations at airports serve to screen for guns. As we saw in Part I, both X-rays and metal detectors have their problems.

An inherent problem with any X-ray device is that any metal object will block it. An X-ray will disclose a gun or bomb in a suitcase, but if there's contraband inside a metal object, it simply won't show. A weapon can easily be hidden inside a piece of machinery. Even pieces of metal will disguise an object. A transistor radio, for example, can hide the components of a bomb. There's no way an X-ray can distinguish between a microchip that is an amplifier and one that is a timer.

VAPOR DETECTORS

The vapor detector is an electronic sniffer that can detect the presence of the fumes that explosives give off. Although these are expensive, they're not exorbitantly high when compared to the approximately thirty thousand dollars it costs to train a dog and handler.

DOGS

There are three types of searches performed by dogs: people, drugs, and explosives. The dogs used are usually German Shepherds, and in the United States most police and military dogs are trained with their handlers at Lackland Air Force Base, near San Antonio, Texas. Dog and handler must train together to be effective, because they work as a team. The course lasts about eight weeks, and at the end the team must "pass" by correctly identifying about 95% of their targets.

Generally, dogs can be trained to seek both people and drugs, both people and explosives, but not both explosives and drugs. The two types of scents are confusing to the dogs, and in practice police and security officers will have "bomb dogs" and/or "narc dogs."

The great advantage of dogs is that they're very fast. A dog can go through an airliner and its baggage in about half an hour. A search team might easily take eight hours to search the plane thoroughly to assure that there's no explosive aboard. This is very important nowadays because of the great number of false bomb threats delivered by phone. The number of phoned in threats is so great that the airlines would face a severe dilemma without dogs. They'd have the choice of delaying flights for extremely long periods or taking an unacceptable risk in sending them off without a search.

Similarly, narc dogs in the hands of police and customs agents can speed up the search for drugs far beyond what it would normally take. Although there are counter-measures to narc dogs, overall their use makes the search for drugs much more efficient.

Police and military dog handlers don't like to publicize this, but dogs are extremely vulnerable. They have a serious weakness in the way they detect, by scent. It's easy to decoy a dog from the hidden material or to disable his sense of smell.

The oldest way is a technique used against "bloodhounds" or tracking dogs, a mixture of dried blood, powder and pepper. A more powerful ingredient was quickly discovered: cocaine. This is a drug which acts as a local anesthetic, and destroys the dog's sense of smell for several hours. Today, there are more powerful and quicker acting local anesthetics available without prescription[1], and mixing one of these with animal blood will attract a dog long enough for him to smell the anesthetic and knock out his smell receptors.

Another technique is to decoy the dog. To hide or mask the scent of a person, it's only necessary to spread some traces of that person's blood or sweat in various odd places. A few drops are all that are needed.

A drug dog is vulnerable to traces of drugs spread around in the area. Marijuana leaves have a very pungent odor, and rubbing them in various places in the area will cause the dog to give so many false alarms that his handler will give up.

A drug dog is especially vulnerable to cocaine. A small amount scattered on the floor will cause the dog to respond to it, and this is the last scent he'll detect for several hours.

Explosives have their characteristic nitrate smells, and bomb dogs home in on these. Rubbing a piece of plastic explosive over luggage will serve as a decoy, especially if it's possible to rub it over luggage belonging to several different people.

Some after-shave lotions will attract a bomb dog, and cause him to come to "alert" as if there were explosives present. This is useful to "mask" the presence of real explosives.

Another approach to defeating detection dogs of both sorts is to eliminate the odor. One way to do this is to place your material in an airtight container. This usually should be metal, as many plastic films will pass volatile nitrate vapors.

The other way to eliminate the characteristic odor is to absorb it, using activated charcoal.[2] You can obtain this in many deodorant products, such as the small canisters placed in refrigerators to kill odors. Gas mask filters usually contain activated charcoal, too, but you can't buy them in supermarkets. They also cost more than odor absorbers.

The technique is to wrap your material tightly in plastic, and then put it in another container with a layer of activated charcoal between your contraband and the outside world. Any trace of odor that comes through will be absorbed by the charcoal.

THE OVERVIEW

With this quick orientation towards the searchers, their outlooks and techniques, you are more familiar than before with what you've got to defeat if you want to keep your secret. Although the searchers may, at first sight, seem terrifyingly effective, they're not as effective as they'd like you to believe. Proof of this exists in the massive drug traffic that crosses our borders, along with the illegal human immigrants. As for items and commodities within our borders, the authorities find them only through the hider's stupidity or extreme bad luck.

NOTES

1. There are various sunburn lotions that contain nupercaine or dibucaine. There are various other anesthetic ointments under various trade names, susch as "Nupercaine," "Orajel," etc. These are all adaptable to the purpose.
2. *Sneak It Through,* Michael Connor, (Boulder, Colorado, Paladin Press, 1984) p. 95.

TOOLS FOR THE JOB

You'll need tools to construct many of the secret compartments you'll see in this book. The essentials are some small "hand tools," but in certain cases power tools will be necessary. This chapter will give you some realistic advice about tools, including a few things you possibly didn't know about them and their uses.

You probably have a number of these tools already. If you don't, you'll have a guide to selecting the ones you will need. Let's start with the simple screwdriver.

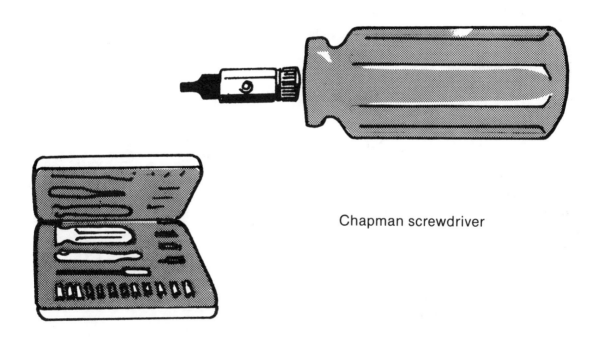

Chapman screwdriver

You may think that a screwdriver is a screwdriver is a screwdriver, but it's not true. The basic requirement in using a screwdriver is that the blade fit the screw closely. Why? Because you don't want to leave marks suggesting tampering. Let's say that you want to hide something in the base of a lamp, and that the base is held on with screws. If you use a poorly fitting blade, you'll gouge and strip the slot, leaving sure signs of tampering to anyone who lifts the lamp and takes a casual look.

A screwdriver should have a blade that's parallel ground. That means that the sides of the blade are parallel, to match the sides of the screw's slot. Tapered blades tend to cam themselves out of the slots when you apply torque.

You'll find it hard to buy parallel ground screwdrivers in your local hardware store. Most of them sell expensive junk in the screwdriver line. What you need is a set of "gunsmith screwdrivers." Two sources for these are:

BROWNELLS, INC.
222 West Liberty, Dept. L
Montezuma, IA 50171
Attn: Frank Brownell III

These people have several sets of gunsmith screwdrivers ranging in price from about twenty to sixty dollars.

HARRY OWEN
PO Box 5337, Dept. L
Hacienda Heights, CA 91745

Harry Owen has the "Chapman" screwdriver set, a compact kit that costs about twenty one dollars and fits in a small flat box. Both Harry Owen's and Brownell's sets have a few Phillips bits in the kit. You probably will need these at some point.

A hammer is useful, if you have the right type. A cast iron or steel hammer is good for driving nails, or with a chisel, but you may find a plastic or leather hammer better for gently tapping the work without leaving marks.

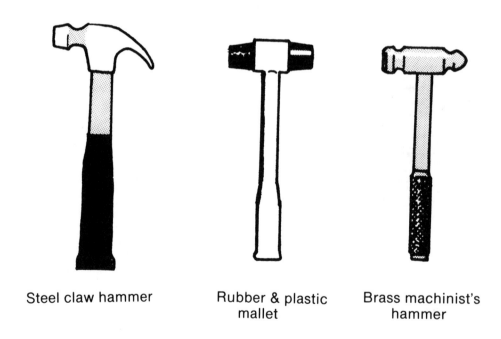

Steel claw hammer   Rubber & plastic   Brass machinist's
                              mallet   hammer

Tapping a secret panel into place is a delicate job, and you don't want to give your secret away by leaving dings. You may also need a machinest's hammer, with a head made of brass. This is for use with punches, as the soft brass doesn't damage the punch.

There are several types of punches. The simple cylindrical punch is for driving out pins. You need this to disassemble certain manufactured items held together with roll pins or taper pins. A machinist's punch has a conical tip to make an indentation for starting a drill bit. An automatic punch is spring loaded. You place the tip where you want the indentation, press down hard, and this cocks a striker against a spring. At the bottom of the stroke, the striker releases, and the blow makes an indentation.

Pin punch

Center punch

Spring-loaded punch

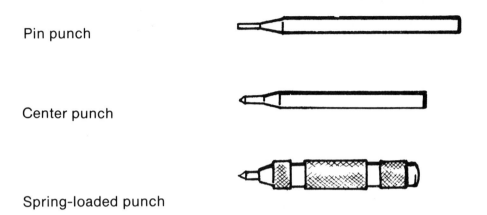

There are basically three types of drills: hand drills, electric drills, and drill presses.

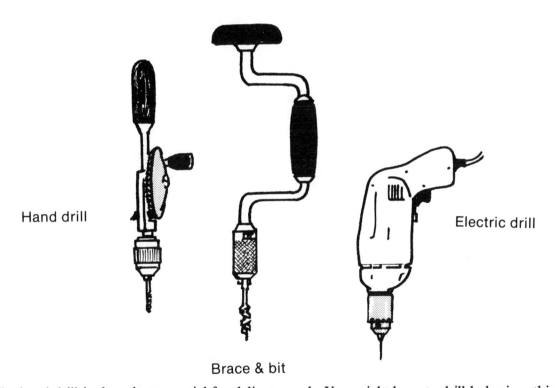

Hand drill

Electric drill

Brace & bit

The hand drill is slow, but essential for delicate work. You might have to drill holes in a thin piece of material, and a power drill might run away with you and you might pierce the other side. This ruins the work if you're trying to conceal something. Best of all, the hand drill has few moving parts and is not affected by a power failure. Also important: it's silent. You may need to drill a hole in very clandestine circumstances one day, and noiseless operation can be a lifesaver.

A brace and bit will come in very handy if you do a lot of work with wood. Get a good set of bits, although these will run you some bucks. They're worth every cent.

The electric drill can be a terrific labor saving device, but only if you get the type best suited for you. Don't waste your time and money with the cheapies, but get one that has a 3/8″ chuck, variable speed, and a reversing feature. This will enable you to drill a number of different materials. Plastic, for example, will melt if you run a drill into it at high speed. Wood will burn with the usual 1750 RPM drilling speed, unless the drill bit is 1/16″ or smaller.

Drilling can be for a simple hole or a threaded hole. With both, you need a steady hand to drill the hole at right angles, and to drill it accurately, without wobbling. If your hand isn't steady enough, you may need a drill press.

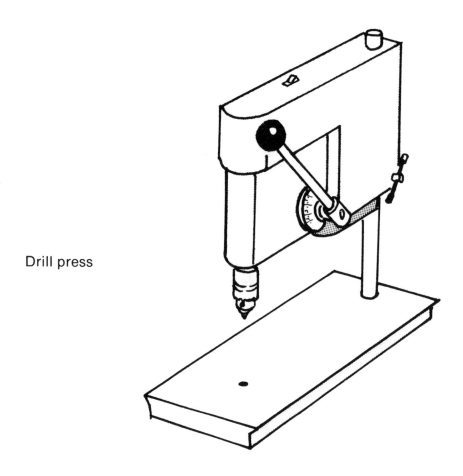

Drill press

This can be expensive, unless you get a used one, or one of the Oriental imports, which run about one hundred dollars. The big advantage of a drill press is that it will drill a hole without the drill's "walking" or going in crooked. You can, with a mechanical table, also do milling and routing, to hollow out some items and machine eccentric cavities.

Router bits are basically side-cutting tools. Don't make the mistake of trying to use a drill bit for side-cutting. It's not designed for that, and although you may get away with it, you'll probably break the bit, unless the material's very soft.

Masonry bit

Router bit

There are three types of drill bits: (1) Carbon steel, (2) high-speed steel, and (3) carbide.

Carbon steel bits are for drilling wood and plastic. High-speed steel bits are for drilling metal, including iron, steel, aluminum, brass and bronze, etc.

Carbide bits use tungsten carbide for the cutting surface, and are for cutting extremely hard substances, such as tool steel. A type of carbide bit that you'll find very useful around the house is the masonry bit.

Twist drill(Carbon and
High-speed steel)

Any sort of stone, masonry, and even wall board is highly abrasive. Even a high quality, high-speed steel drill bit can be ruined after drilling one hole in wall board. A masonry bit has long-wearing carbide cutting edges, and will drill through masonry without premature wear.

Using drills is an art as well as a science. Some points to watch are:

● Use the right speed. If you see smoke coming from the work, or it starts to melt, something's wrong. You're probably going too fast. If the drill tends to catch in the work, you're probably drilling at too slow a rotation. Larger diameter drill bits usually require a slower speed than smaller ones.

● Don't jam the drill into the work. Excessive force will increase friction without speeding up the work, and can break the bit.

● Make sure your drill is sharp. Examine it with a magnifier if necessary. Many people waste time, tear up the work, and generally make a mess of it trying to use a dull bit.

● Use a lubricant when drilling metal, except when drilling iron. A light oil, such as WD-40 or Leading Edge, will ease drilling a lot. Use very little.

If you want to make a threaded hole, you'll need a tap to cut the threads. You'll also need to drill the right sized hole. Hardware stores have pocket charts listing the drills to use for tapped holes of various sizes.

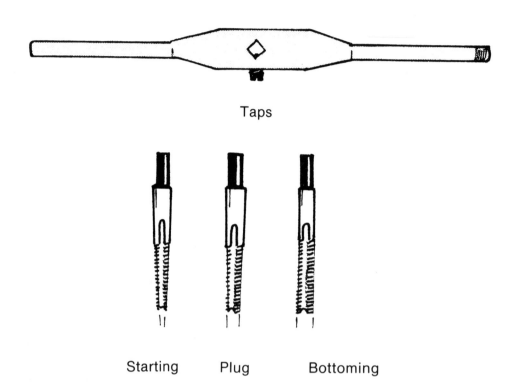

Taps

Starting   Plug   Bottoming

Taps generally are made of high-speed steel. Be careful when buying taps. If they're not high-speed steel, don't buy. They're junk.

There are three types of taps: (1) Starting taps, with a long taper on the threads, (2) plug taps, with a medium taper, and (3) bottoming taps, with almost no taper. Be sure to use the right type or you'll have endless trouble. A starting tap is just that, a tap with a long taper for easy starting into a drilled hole. A plug tap has a short taper. It isn't as easy to start in a hole unless you have a machine fixture, but it's almost an all purpose tap. It's harder to use, so be careful. Both starting and plug taps will serve well for through holes.

A bottoming tap has practically no taper. It's for tapping a blind hole right to the bottom. You always need to start the hole with a starting or plug tap before using a bottoming tap.

Tip: Always use lubricant when using a tap. Use plenty, to carry off the chips and prevent galling.

Files, both wood and metal, are almost always necessary. You'll see a confusing variety of files in a well stocked hardware store. Whatever you do, don't buy a set. Buy just one or two for the specific purpose you have in mind.

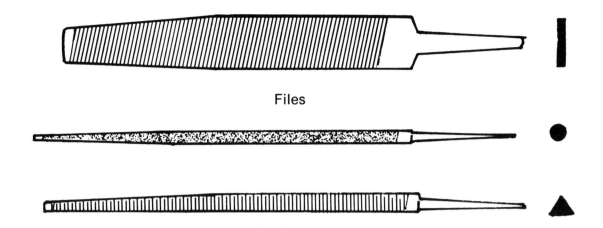

Files

One important point about using a file: Always stroke forward, never backward. The teeth are set to cut in one direction only, and going in reverse can dull or break them. Always use the file in a suitable handle, and occasionally brush it off to prevent loading the teeth with material, which only increases friction and reduces efficiency.

Unless you have a heavy cutting job to do, use a fine file. You need to leave no traces of your work, and a fine finish on your work helps.

Chisels are for cutting cavities in wood. A set of chisels will be essential for creating hiding places in doors, molding, and furniture. Don't skimp on these. Buy the best you can afford. A set of three should do for most purposes. The sizes you'll find most useful are ½″, ¾″, and 1″.

Using chisels is mainly an art. Practice thoroughly on scrap wood before using these for real.

A rivet tool is important for certain work. You may have to take apart something held together with rivets, then replace the rivets. You may also choose to replace screws with rivets, to discourage disassembly by a searcher.

The most useful type is the pop rivet tool. This lets you insert a rivet from one side. A supply of rivets of different diameters will round out your rivet kit.

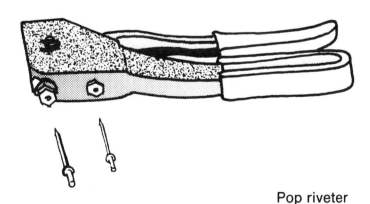

Pop riveter

Pliers are simple, yet oft neglected tools. A pair of ordinary pliers starts you off, but a pair of parallel jaw pliers is even more useful, especially as one type has a wire cutter built into one of the jaws. These are called "outside cutting pliers," and you can get them from Brownell, listed on page 16.

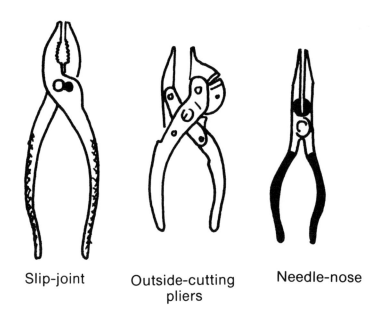

Slip-joint   Outside-cutting   Needle-nose
pliers

Don't forget needle-nose pliers for those tight fits.

Channel-lock pliers are useful for quickly taking apart plumbing, but a basin wrench is better and more versatile in tight spots.

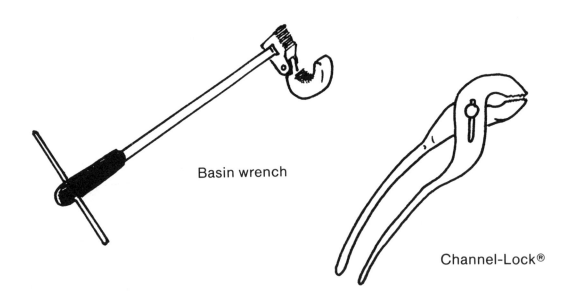

Basin wrench

Channel-Lock®

A set of crescent wrenches is useful and versatile, because it can serve for a number of different sized nuts, including large plumbing fixtures. The advantage of using wrenches is that you don't leave tool marks, a sure giveaway to a searcher. Your crescent wrenches should cover a range of sizes, from about ¼″ up to two inches, for plumbing applications.

Crescent wrenches aren't quite the best for precision work. There may be difficulty getting the wrench into tight spots and if the jaws open up at all, you can mar the nut with slight slippage and camming.

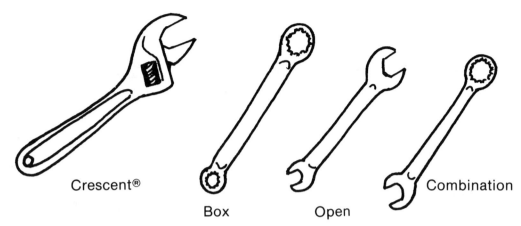

Crescent® Box Open Combination

Invest in a set of box and open-end wrenches, if your work is going to involve machine screws, bolts, and nuts. You may be creating secret hiding places in a car or truck, and these wrenches will be essential for that use. The sort that has a box wrench on one end and an open-end type on the other is the most versatile. Sears and Roebuck has an excellent set.

For electronic chassis work, a set of nut drivers is important. These let you get into confined spaces where you can't swing a wrench.

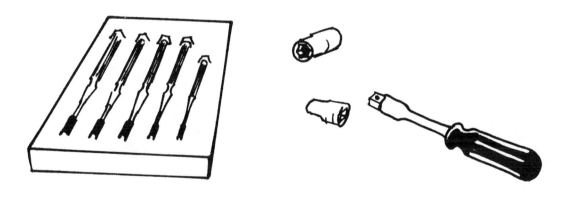

Large & Small nutdrivers

A cheap set will do here. If you intend to do a lot of work with them, though, get a more expensive heavy-duty set. The cheapies won't stand up.

Hex wrenches can also come in handy. These are sometimes known as "Allen wrenches." If you use them only occasionally, a very inexpensive set will do. For frequent use, a set of ball-end hex wrenches will be very convenient. One eleven piece set, covering sizes from .050″ up to 5/16″, is made by "Bondhus" and is available in tool supply stores.

A wood saw and a hacksaw are essential. For cutting wood, carbon steel will do. Buy only high speed blades for your hacksaw, though. Remember, lift the blade from the work when you bring it back. Don't strike the teeth against the work backwards.

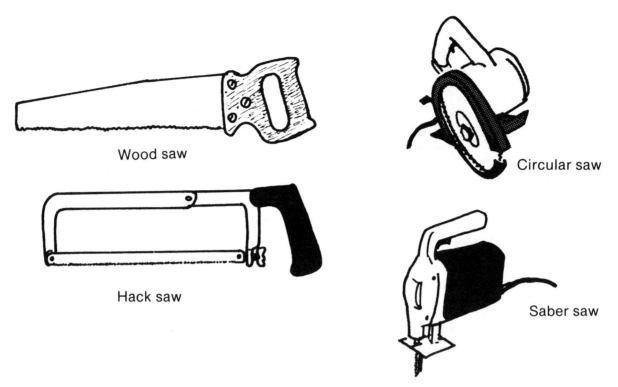

Wood saw

Circular saw

Hack saw

Saber saw

Generally, a power table saw won't be necessary. You'd need one if you were building furniture, or doing other heavy-duty work, but for this light application, a light saber saw or circular saw will do well.

A utility knife often comes in handy. The razor blade type is best, because you may have to do some fine work, such as cutting panels out of carpet without leaving a trace of cutting. An X-Acto knife lets you get into tight places.

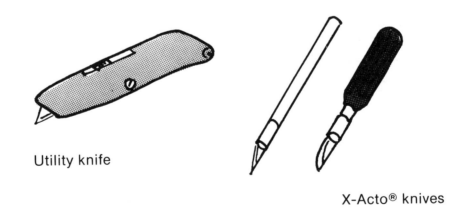

Utility knife

X-Acto® knives

A soldering iron can be handy if you need to modify electronic components or seal material into food cans. You can use the "pencil" type of soldering iron for electronic work, but the "pistol" type will be better able to handle heavy-duty applications.

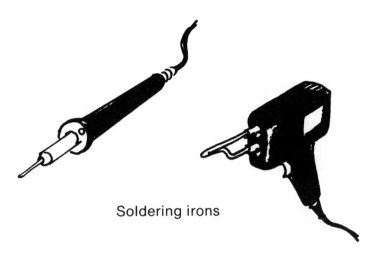

Soldering irons

A propane torch will be necessary for very heavy-duty soldering, such as when you hide things in an auto muffler. An assortment of solder types will round out your set.

A miter box is handy for cutting angles when doing woodworking. If you need to install replacement sections of baseboard, and other wood components, you'll need one of these.

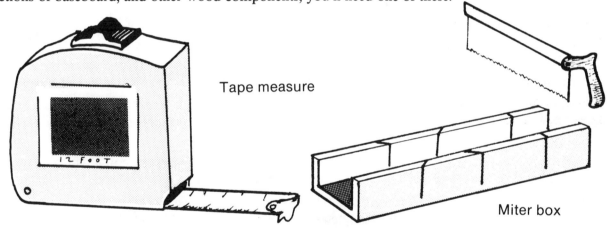

Tape measure

Miter box

A tape measure is also necessary. It's light, cheap, has few moving parts, and a power failure won't knock you out.

Sandpaper in various grits, emery paper, crocus cloth, and number 600 wet-and-dry are all finishing tools. You may not think of these at first, but you'd better have a few on hand when you need them. Don't forget a short piece of two by four to serve as a sanding block.

Assorted paints and paint brushes are essential for certain finishing operations. It's impossible to predict what you're going to need until you need it.

Glue is very important. Glue can be a lifesaver.

First is wood glue. Elmer's is a good casein glue for working with wood. The problem with most wood glues is that they can loosen in dampness.

Epoxy is extremely versatile, but has a couple of special characteristics worth noting. First, it will fill space, unlike some other glues. This is because epoxy has mechanical strength of its own, unlike many glues that can only adhere to other materials in close contact. Epoxy is also versatile because it accepts fillers, such as glass fiber, sand, talc, and other materials to add bulk and help fill space.

Epoxy glue always comes in two parts, resin and hardener. It needs mixing immediately before use, and has a "pot life" of between one minute and one-half hour, depending on the type. The five-minute epoxies must be used immediately, because they start to set as soon as you mix them. The regular epoxies have longer times before they start setting, but also take much longer to set and develop maximum strength. This can be up to twenty four hours.

Surfaces must be clean, dry, and free of oil when using epoxy. Temperature is also important. Epoxy simply won't set in cold temperatures.

One other use for epoxy is to fabricate fake electronic components. We'll cover this in the appropriate chapter, but here let's note that the best epoxy kit for this is the "Acraglas Gel," from Brownell. This kit has a gel-type epoxy which does not run, and a small envelope of brown dye which colors the epoxy to match many electronic components.

Cyanoacrylate is also known as "super glue" or "crazy glue," and is remarkable in its properties. Generally, it will set within a minute or two, upon contact with air. It's useful only in thin layers, as it has no mechanical strength. For this reason, it doesn't work well sticking to porous surfaces. It works well with metal, glass, some plastics, and some hardwoods. A drop is all you need for most uses.

The biggest problem with super glue is waste. Tubes are very bad containers because the glue starts to dry out as soon as you open the tube. The best container for practical use of super glue is the "Gluematic Pen," made by Duro. This costs slightly more than the tube, but it's a bargain because a spring-loaded applicator valve meters out only what you need. You simply press it down on the surface you want to glue to release the glue.

One extremely important use of epoxy is to use on screws and bolts you don't want opened. In some instances, you may want to discourage disassembly by searchers. One good way to do this is to persuade them that the screw or bolt is "frozen." A drop of epoxy on the threads will make a screw, bolt, or nut almost impossible to remove. So will a drop of "LOK-TITE" Red Label thread compound.

If you've glued the threads, how do you get them open? One way is heat. Playing a propane torch on the threads will break down the epoxy. Another way is to use an epoxy solvent. Acetone will do in a pinch.

Other types of glue which will help in certain cases are "Contact" cement, household cement, and airplane glue. The advantage of "Contact" cement is that it's flexible.

Another chemical that comes in handy is instant cold gun blue. This is either a liquid or a paste, and it puts a dark blue finish on ferrous metals, and a deep gray or black finish on various alloys. This is useful for eliminating the shine of bright metal after reworking to install a secret compartment.

A spray can of auto undercoat is especially useful when covering up the installation of a hidden compartment on the underside of a car. It doesn't really matter if the car's already undercoated or not. This spray goop resembles grease and after a couple of miles of driving it will have road film to help it blend in perfectly.

Having the tools is half the job. Using them is the other. That's what the rest of this book's about.

LOOKING FOR HIDING PLACES:
A WAY OF THINKING

Your most powerful weapon, your most useful tool, is between your ears. An alert, agile mind will help you more than a strong pair of hands. Use your eyes and common sense, and you'll have done the most important part of the job.

Seeking hiding places requires a shift in your point of view. Instead of looking at and thinking of objects as filling space, you have to think of the empty spaces inside and behind them, the wasted space, the unused space.

Most of the objects we see and use each day are either hollow, or have space that we can hollow out to make hiding places. There are four things we have to keep in mind when we look at something with intent to create a hiding place:

(1) Size. Is there enough space to hide what we want to hide? Be mentally flexible here. Don't just look at the hiding place. Look also at the object you wish to hide. Think about disassembling it, or breaking it up into smaller lots. Consider a weapon such as a handgun, for example. A full-size auto pistol measures about seven inches long by five high. You can reduce these dimensions by field-stripping it if you have to smuggle it. Removing the slide and barrel will allow you to pack the frame into a smaller space. You can hide the slide, barrel, mainspring, and magazine separately. Cartridges can be hidden separately, if necessary.

(2) Is it obvious? Hiding something in a drawer is obvious. Taping an envelope to the underside of a drawer is less so. This is because a drawer is designed with empty space to hold objects. Hiding something inside an apparently solid object, such as drilling out a bureau leg, is not obvious. Disguising the form of the object or material you wish to hide also reduces its visibility.

(3) Workmanship is important. The most cleverly conceived secret compartment is useless if sloppy workmanship leaves tool marks to betray it to the casual observer. Even the most dull, brutish, and insensitive cop can spot a hide when there are obvious seams and cracks showing. A searcher who picks up an apparently solid object and hears a rattle inside will surely become suspicious.

(4) You have to keep in mind the special characteristics of what you're trying to hide. Is it temperature sensitive, as are undeveloped film, some chemicals and drugs, and ammunition? Heat will degrade these, and your hiding place mustn't expose them to excessive heat.

Is the material sensitive to water damage? This can preclude burial, unless you use waterproofing.

Is the material resistant to certain chemicals and vapors? A gun barrel won't be damaged by immersion in a gasoline tank, but ammunition will.

Anything metallic is vulnerable to detection by metal detectors, unless it's hidden in something made of metal, such as a car.

HOW MUCH WORK IS INVOLVED?

Some hiding places are "naturals," with little or no work needed to make them serviceable. You can wrap a package of money in aluminum foil and hide it in your freezer. You can tape an envelope under a drawer. You can hide small objects such as jewels in a layer of cooking grease at the bottom of a pot.[1]

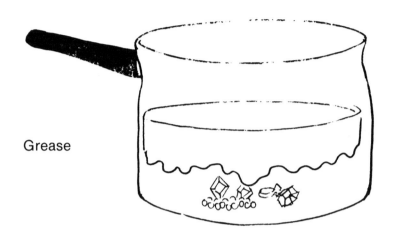

Grease

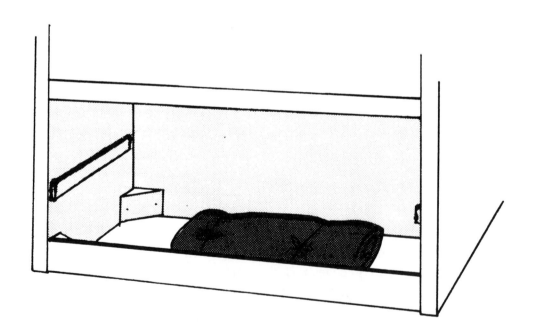

"Hidden" space under bottom drawer

The space under the bottom drawer in a cabinet is another easy to use hiding place.[2]

Loose bricks in a wall or fireplace can serve to cover hiding places.

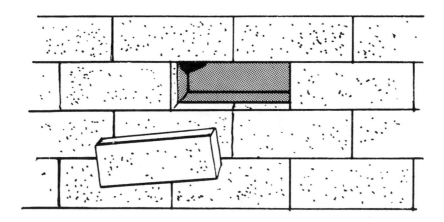

Space behind bricks

A transistor radio's battery compartment can hold a battery, or something else. Some also have compartments to hold earplugs.

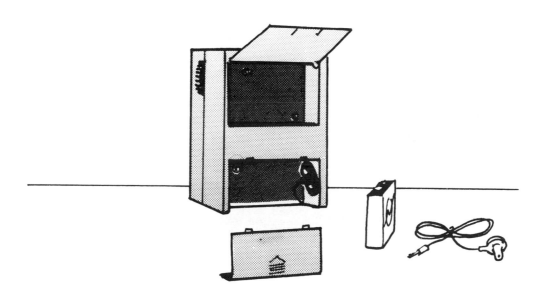

Transistor radio

An attic full of glass fiber insulation serves as a natural hiding place.[3]

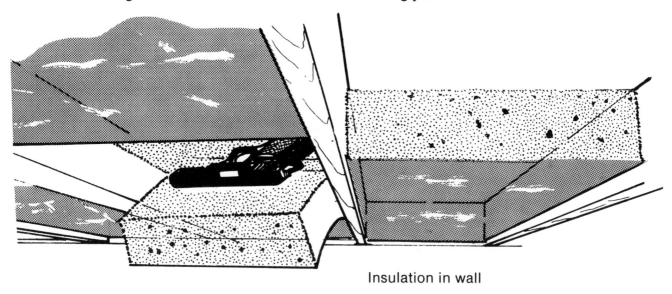

Insulation in wall

A great advantage of using glass fiber insulation is that anyone rummaging through it will pick up broken ends of glass fibers in his skin. If your mind runs in a sadistic vein, you can make good use of this fact. Go up to your attic and purposely disturb the insulation so that any searcher will become suspicious. You might also place a few innocuous packages underneath, to compel a searcher to follow through. By the time he's ripped up your attic, he'll have a hide full of glass fibers and an itch that won't quit!

These few examples will give you an inkling of the science and art of creating hidey holes. We'll progress from the easy-to-build ones to the more elaborate. Let's stop here for a moment, and go to the kitchen for a beer.

NOTES

1. *How To Hide Anything,* Michael Connor, (Boulder, Colorado, Paladin Press, 1984) p. 13.

2. *Hidden Riches,* Chas. M. Albano, (Tacoma, Washington, Erco, Inc., 1974) p. 15.

3. *How To Hide Anything,* p. 22.

SIMPLE JOBS AT HOME

No matter how clever you are, no matter how diligently you plan, no matter how carefully you work, anything you hide will be found if the searcher puts enough time and effort into it. We've noted that counter-espionage police, such as Scotland Yard's Special Branch, the FBI, and the KGB, search very thoroughly. If ever one of them gets on your case, their people will come into your home and take it apart down to the last nail.

However, cleverness will often defeat less adept searchers. Let's survey your home and look for places to hide things, places that won't require much work, or especially skilled work.

FURNITURE

Believe it or not, most of your furniture is empty space. Most of the rest can be hollowed out to create hiding places. Let's start with a wooden stool, or a wooden leg of a chair. Drilling a deep hole to hold small items requires only a drill, and a set of replacement feet. You should drill out all four legs, and replace all four feet, to make them match.[1] Keep in mind that you don't want to make the holes so large that you weaken the legs excessively. It could be very embarrassing if a visitor sat on the chair and it collapsed under him, revealing a roll of bills in the hollow leg.

Upholstered furniture is even easier to rework. Work loose the cloth covering the underside of your sofa or easy chair. The cushioning provides ample space to conceal anything from a jewel to a weapon. Replace the cloth, and fasten it the same way.[2]

Stereo speakers are mostly empty space. You can open them to hide small to medium objects with hardly any problems. Today it's easier than before, because many are made with panels held on with Velcro, and these are easy to remove and replace.[3]

Drawers, whether kitchen or bureau, offer you the chance to insert false bottoms. Use the same material as the real bottom, and hold it in place with Velcro or a set of plastic strip magnets, which you can buy in hardware stores or notion shops.[4]

False bottoms in drawers are useful only for hiding flat or small objects, such as documents, money, and jewels. But while you're hiding these goodies, make sure you fasten them so that they don't rattle.

The bureau itself can give you the opportunity to construct a secret compartment. Often, there's a space between the top of the bureau and the top drawer. There are two ways you can handle this. You can construct a box inside that does not interfere with the drawer, and arrange the top panel to lift off, or you can simply construct a removable false bottom. The top panel attaches with magnetic or friction snaps.

If you have brass candlesticks, lamp bases, and other items of furniture made of cast metal, keep in mind that most of these were cast hollow to save on the cost of metal. They have built-in secret compartments often simply covered by felt glued to their bottoms. With a razor blade, cut through the layer of glue and explore the compartment. If you decide to use it, you can reglue the felt to close it, or you can use Velcro to keep the felt in place.[5]

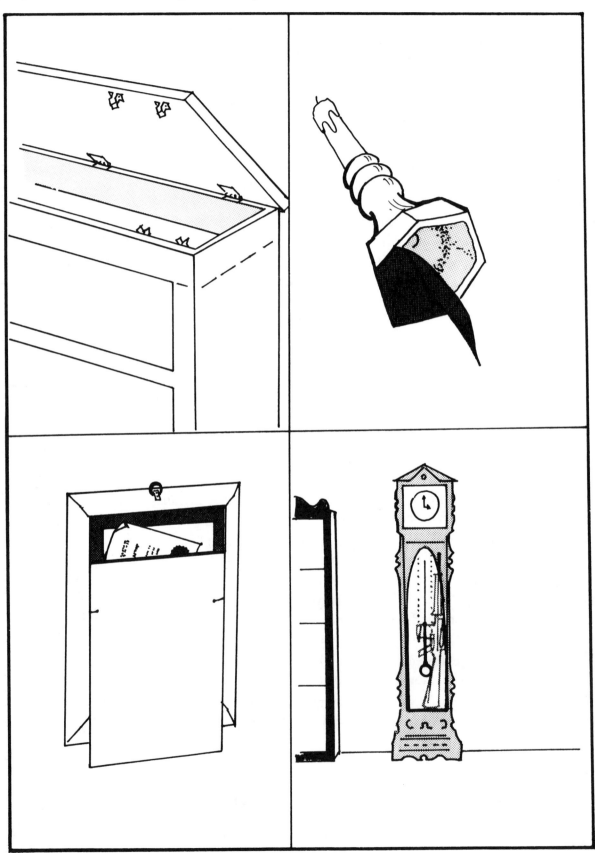

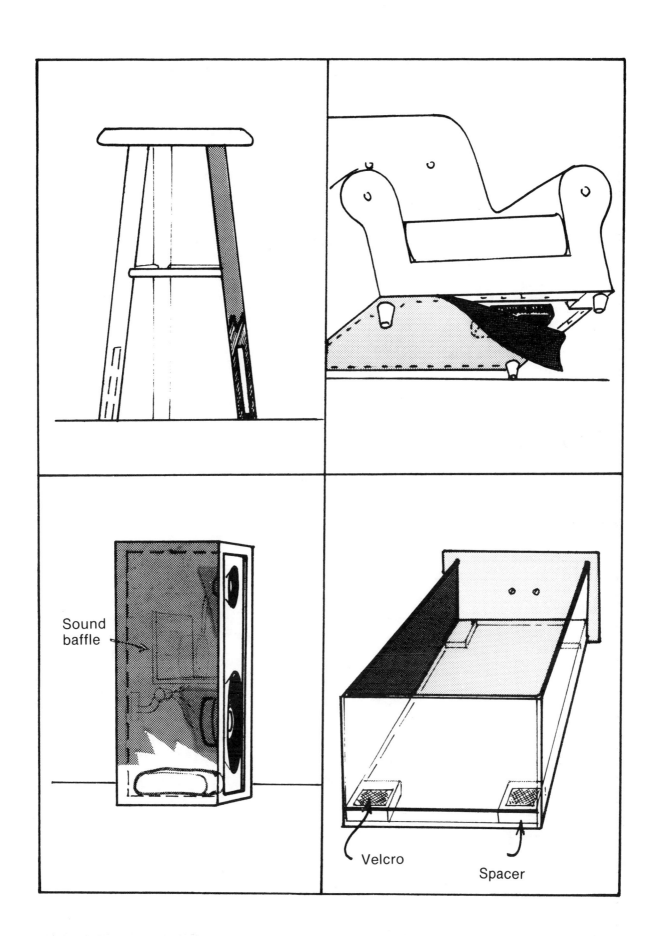

Sound baffle

Velcro

Spacer

Picture frames are always good for hiding flat objects. They always have several layers of cardboard held in by glue or nails. Prying these out and inserting documents, money, or microfilm in the back will work.[6]

Old clocks, especially grandfather clocks, usually have some dead space you can exploit.[7] These are already built secret compartments, accessible simply by removing the back.

Flower pots serve as hiding places for small objects stored inside plastic 35mm film canisters. These plastic canisters are watertight, and allow you to store ammunition, drugs, and other fragile and sensitive goods inside.[8]

Pianos have many unobtrusive spaces. So do sewing machines.[9] You can take advantage of these to hide small to medium objects.

NOTES

1. *How To Hide Anything,* Michael Connor, (Boulder, Colorado, Paladin Press, 1984) p. 3.

2. *Ibid.,* p. 2.

3. *Ibid.,* p. 4.

4. *Ibid.,* p. 7.

5. *Hidden Riches,* Chas. M. Albano, (Tacoma, Washington, Erco, Inc., 1974) p. 17.

6. *Search!,* James R. Warnke, (Boynton Beach, Florida, James R. Warnke Publishing, 1982) p. 50.

7. *Ibid.,* p. 52.

8. *Ibid.,* p. 52.

9. *Ibid.,* p. 58.

HIDING PLACES IN THE HOME: STRUCTURES AND COMPARTMENTS

Seemingly solid structures in your home are, in reality, mostly empty space. Let's examine the possibilities. We'll find that, in some instances, we can hide things with very little work. In others, we'll have to make a determined and skillful effort.

WALLS

Interior walls are usually "sheet rock" nailed over 2″ x 4″ studs spaced from 16″ to 25″ apart, depending on how closely the local building code is enforced and on whether the wall is a load bearing one or not. The building's electrical wiring and plumbing run within these walls. The net result is that practically all walls provide compartments four inches deep by over a foot wide by eight feet high. Occasionally, you'll find insulation within walls.

There are natural accesses to the interior of these walls. Practically all rooms have light switch plates and electrical outlets. Each box has a metal or plastic housing and a cover plate.

Before starting work, be sure to turn off the power at the main box. *Heed this warning.* While many of us have sustained shocks from house current without fatal results, repeated carelessness can cause your luck to run out. Another hazard is that all modern houses are also wired for 220 volts, as air conditioners, washers and dryers use this voltage.

All of these electrical boxes have cover plates. Removing these allows the insertion of material behind them. Use a screwdriver, but be sure that the blade's a perfect fit in the slot. You don't want to mar the surface! Leaving marks is amateurish, and provides a searcher unmistakable signs of tampering. If you find that you've left gouges, cover them up with a coat of paint. Many sloppy householders who do their own painting cover the entire electrical face plate because they're too sloppy to remove it before painting and reattach it when finished. Another good point about painting over screw heads is that it makes disassembly more difficult. Consider this if you intend to leave your material hidden for a long time. Think of an alternative method of attachment if you need ready access.

There are several ways to create hiding places.

The simplest is to hide objects inside the electrical box itself.[1] You should insulate any metallic objects in order not to cause a hazard. Another way is to remove the box and build a shelf behind and under it. This will hold small objects.

How do you hold the shelf? You could, of course, drive a couple of nails through the wallboard but this would require using putty and paint to disguise the nail holes. A simpler way is epoxy. Make sure your shelf is a close fit so that it holds by friction while the epoxy sets. This should not be hard, because a piece of 2″ x 4″ should fit perfectly. You'll find that the size of the objects you can hide this way will be sharply limited because of the size of the access hole.

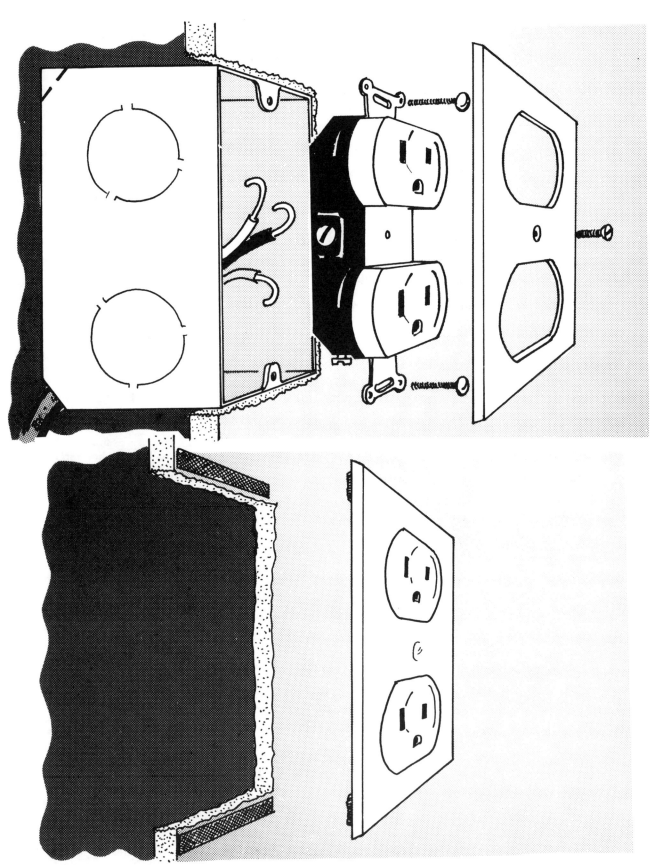

Another way is to construct dummy outlets. For this, you don't use the entire outlet box, just the face plates. You do have to remove the plug faces from the guts and glue them into the slots in the face plates. Use plastic cement, super glue, or epoxy. Super glue and plastic cement will work best because they set very quickly, and you don't need tremendous load bearing strength. Cut off the screw heads and attach them to the face plate with epoxy and super glue. You won't be using these to attach the plate to the wall, anyway, because you'd then need a screw hole for each one, which means a box, which means restricting your space. Paint over the screw heads to deter removal. This gives you the best of both worlds. You have quick access, and a searcher is discouraged.

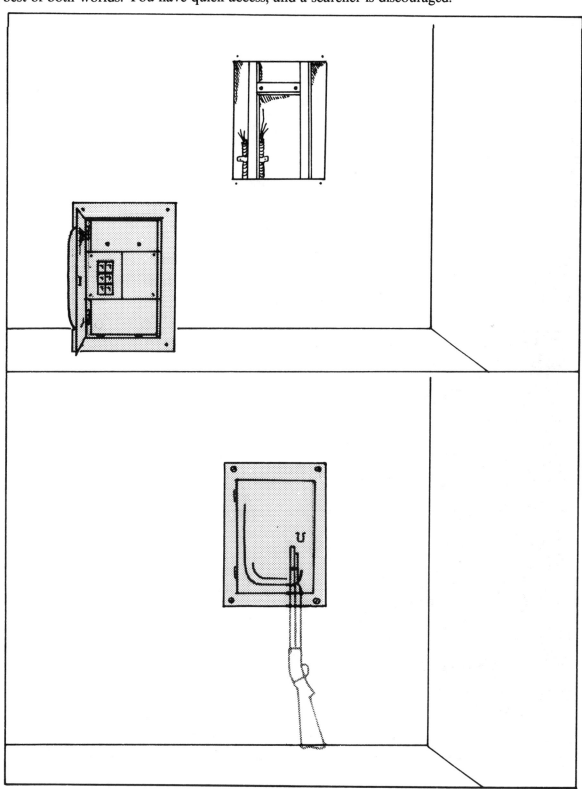

Cut a hole in the wall slightly smaller than the face plate. Construct your hiding place behind it, and attach a couple of Velcro buttons at the corners. Matching Velcro buttons on the face plate will enable you to hold it in place.

Your best bet is to use whatever space there is behind and inside switch plates. If you install a dummy switch, you may arouse suspicion because it obviously won't work, and anyone trying it will wonder why. Few people come into your home and plug in appliances, and the risk of discovery is consequently far less.

Don't overlook the possibilities in outside boxes. A main box on your outside wall, or a fuse box in the basement can provide more concealment space than a small outlet box.[2]

Main electrical boxes, especially those on exterior walls, usually have hasps for locking. Make use of these. A padlock will make a searcher's job harder.

Examine your fuse box. How is it held on? Usually, there will be several screw heads in the back panel. Remove these and inspect the wall behind. If it's an interior wall, it's already hollow. An outside wall may need a little work, removing bricks or drilling holes in slump blocks.

Because a fuse box is larger, it can conceal a larger access hole. This enables you to build a substantial hide. You may even have enough space to swing a rifle through the aperture.

Telephone outlets are also useful for caching small items. Recently built houses are usually pre-wired, with at least one telephone outlet plate in each room. The owner removes the plate and installs an outlet socket if he wishes an extension in that room. If you've just moved into a new house, save any covers you replace. You can use these to cover new hides. The beauty of these is that they require much less work than other sorts of hides, because there's only a blank plate, with no outlet holes, or with one small center hole. You have to dispose of far fewer "guts" in creating your hide.

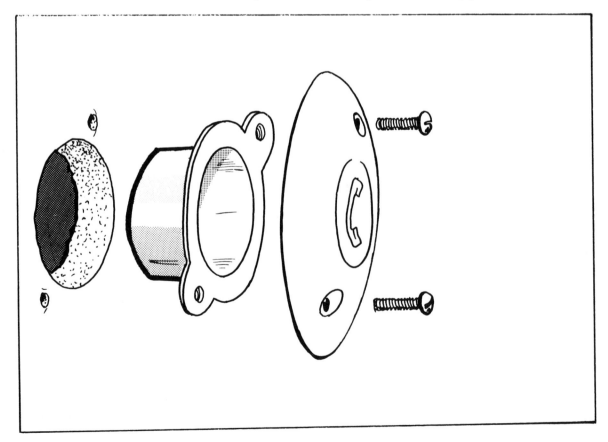

You can also use telephone outlets as hiding places, in the same way as you use electrical outlets.

Ceiling lights often provide handy prospects for concealment. Unscrew the base of each one you have and inspect the interior. Usually, there's an electrical box about four inches round, with mounting holes for the screws holding the light. Turn off the current first.

Often, the base plate is much larger than the electrical box. This lets you conceal material inside it, or to cover a larger hole. One limitation is that the electrical box for a ceiling light is usually attached to a ceiling beam, because it must hold the weight of the light. This cramps your space because you can only use one side. If the ceiling fixture is made to hold a ceiling fan, it will surely be securely attached to a main beam. If you live in a single story building and have a ceiling fixture, inspect the attic before starting any work at all. You may find that the space behind the fixture is completely exposed.

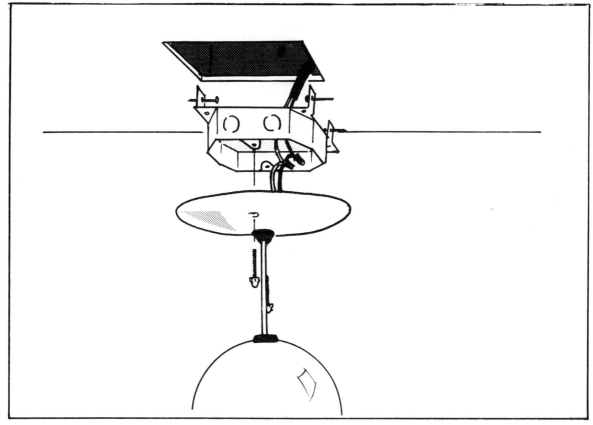

AIR DUCTS

An air heating and cooling system allows a lot of work with the ducts. First, the grills are usually held with two screws, which allows fairly easy access.

Removing the screws will allow you to store fairly large objects inside, where they'll be hidden from a casual look-see. Some searchers may take a look through the grill with a flashlight, and defeating this requires you to store your material farther in.

If you need quick access, there's a variation. You may find this worthwhile if you're concealing a weapon which you may need urgently for self-defense. Remove the screws, cut off the heads, and epoxy them into the chambered holes. Paint the grill to discourage attempts at unscrewing it. Attach hinges to one side to allow you to swing the grill open quickly.[3] You'll want to be careful to have the grill flush against the wall, without a telltale gap.

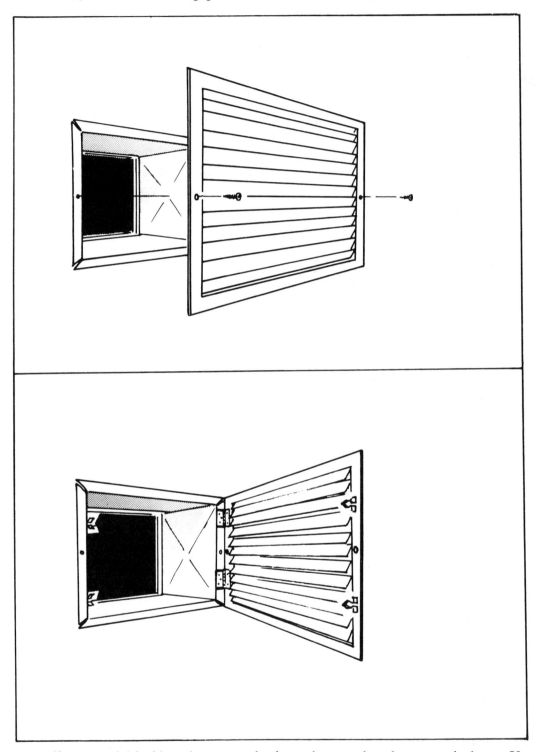

When concealing material inside a duct, use a horizontal run rather than a vertical one. You don't want to risk dropping objects down out of reach.[4] If necessary, use magnets to hold light material, such as paper, so that it doesn't blow against and block the grill.

If you need more space, you can construct a dummy grill. For this, you need only to obtain a grill to match the others, and cut a hole in the wallboard to accept it. Use a screw or hinge arrangement.

This will allow a large aperture into the wall, enough to pass long objects. One possible problem will arise if a searcher inspects your ductwork. He may wonder why there is no duct leading to that grill.

If you need still more space, construct dummy ductwork. In many houses, the garage isn't air conditioned or heated, and you can build a dummy duct from the central duct to this remote point. This allows you a lot of latitude, because when you hide material in the other ducts, you must be careful not to obstruct them. You can pack a dummy duct chock full.

For this, you have to procure sections of duct to match the existing ductwork. Solder or epoxy the sections together to fit. You may decide that you want a grill at the end of the duct. A casual search, as in the case of a burglary, will not uncover the deception, but a more thorough searcher might wonder why there is a duct running into a room which lacks an outlet.

A fine point to watch is to run the duct on top of and across ceiling beams, if you're going to store heavy material inside. Weight can become important, and you must keep in mind that ordinary ceilings are not made to support weight. If you must run the duct between two beams, use metal straps attached to the beams to support the weight.

Cover the traces of your work by emptying your vacuum cleaner bag over the new ductwork. Do this several times, to ensure that a thick layer of dust covers everything.

PLUMBING

Many bathrooms have access holes under the sink. These are usually covered with a six inch chromed disc, held in place by a central screw. This access hole is to permit a snake to be inserted into a main drain for unplugging. This is a ready made hiding place.

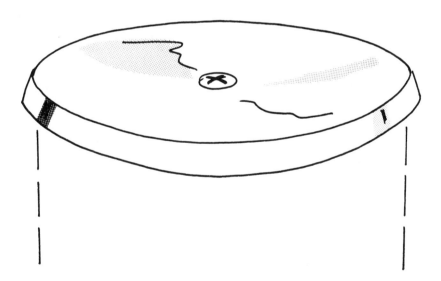

If you don't have one, install one. Cut a hole in the wall for your hide, and have a chromed disc ready to cover it. Cut the head off the screw that would normally hold it in place, and glue the head into the central chamfer of the plate. Super glue or epoxy will do.

A floor drain is useful for those who have basements or garages. If the drain is real, it will still serve to hide small objects. You can do this by using a waterproof bag hung from the inside of the drainpipe.[5]

If you don't have one, you're better off. You probably don't need one, and this means that when you construct your fake one, you run far less risk of having your valuables drowned. A post hole digger is your main tool, once you've broken through concrete with a pick axe. Once you've dug your hole as deep as you can, you obtain a section of pipe to fit. Cap the end of the pipe. This will be the bottom of your secret compartment. Drill a couple of holes in opposite sides at the top end of the pipe for a rope handle. Obtain a grating and mount somewhat larger than the diameter of the pipe you've chosen, and cement this in place. If you feel that there's a risk of flooding, you'll want to cut a plastic lid for your pipe to protect the contents. Hold this down with four or more screws around the diameter of the pipe, using an O-ring or gasket to seal it.

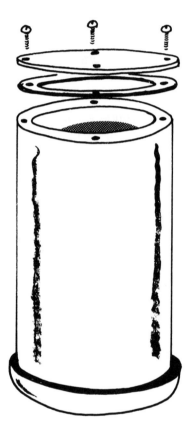

Once the concrete is dry, check to see if it matches the rest. It probably won't. You have two ways to disguise your work. The simpler is a heavy coat of crud, the grungier the better. The second, and neater, way is a coat of paint. Many people paint concrete floors, and this will help conceal the fact that your paint job's concealing an alteration.

False pipes are among the easiest to install. This is a much more secure method of hiding than placing objects in toilet tanks.[6] Logical places for sections of fake pipes are the kitchen, bathroom, and basement. Ideally, a fake pipe should be between two opposite walls in a room. This gives the appearance of each end being firmly anchored in or through a wall and dissuades closer examination. Searchers sometimes will unscrew the drain itself. A single length of pipe, with no visible seams or other interruptions, will seem inaccessible.

To set up such a pipe, you need to make holes in the two walls. One hole should be fairly deep. This lets you insert the end of the pipe deeply into it to allow you to swing the other end into place and into the shallow hole in the opposite wall.

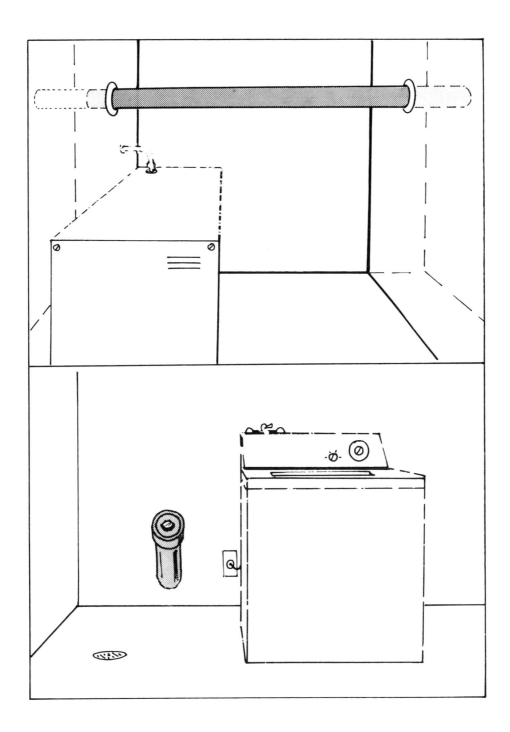

A variation on this is the fake waste stack or fake cleanout plug.[7] These need be only a couple of feet long, and embedded into existing concrete floors. If there's no basement, a cleanout plug can be in the wall of the house or sticking out of the wall, under a sink. Normally, if the sink's free standing, a chromed cover plate will hide the cleanout plug, as previously described. If the plug is in a cabinet, as in the kitchen or bathroom, it may easily be exposed. If the plug's in the laundry or utility room, under the utility sink, it will surely be exposed.

Water heaters have heavy insulation between their outer shells and the water tanks. There are usually access plates if the thermostats are between the two shells. The better heaters have two thermostats, and two access plates.

How much work do you want to put into a hiding place? As we've already seen, some of them require heavy labor. Next, we'll cover more ambitious ones, which require more work and skill.

NOTES

1. *Secret Hiding Places,* Charles Robinson, (Cornville, Arizona, Desert Publications, 1981) pp. 13-14.

2. *Search!,* James R. Warnke, (Boynton Beach, Florida, James R. Warnke Publishing, 1982) pp. 85-87.

3. *How To Hide Anything,* Michael Connor, (Boulder, Colorado, Paladin Press, 1984) p. 21.

4. *Secret Hiding Places,* pp. 56-57.

5. *How To Hide Almost Anything,* David Krotz, (New York, William Morrow and Company, 1975) p. 62.

6. *How to Hide Anything,* pp. 23-39.

7. *Secret Hiding Places,* pp. 33-34.

HIDING PLACES IN THE HOME:
STRUCTURES AND COMPARTMENTS
PART II

DOORS

Practically all interior doors and many modern exterior doors are of hollow-core construction. This makes the task of hiding material inside much easier than before. The obvious place to construct an access to a secret compartment in a door is at the top.[1] The method is simple.

Because hollow-core doors are cheaply made sandwiches of wood veneer and cardboard, it's usually only necessary to cut into the top of the door with a utility knife. This will expose a deep compartment, the hollow core of the door. This will serve as a hiding place for money, documents, drugs, ammunition, and various other licit and illicit materials.

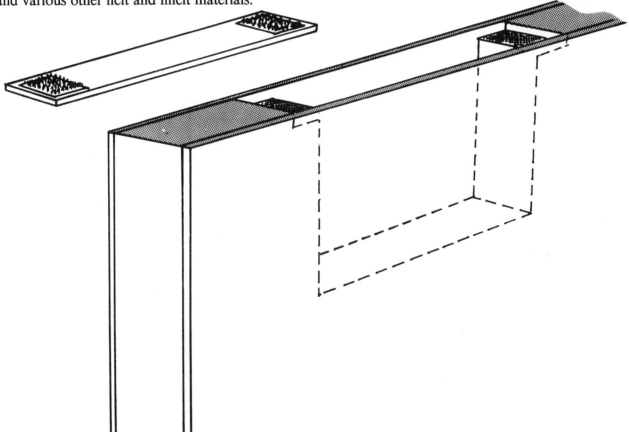

To finish the job, you make a lid of thin wood, or even cardboard painted to match, resting it on steps inside the compartment so that it's flush with the sides of the door. A couple of small strip magnets or Velcro will hold it securely enough.

If the door you intend to use as a hiding place is solid, you'll have to drill and chisel out your compartment. Finish the job as described above.

The door jamb offers a somewhat roomier hiding place. It's much more secure. It's also much harder to build. You start by removing the stop molding from the top of the door frame.[2]

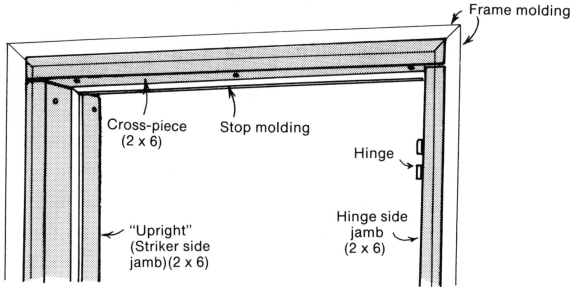

This allows you to pry the vertical woodwork on the lock striker side away from the wall. Once you remove this, you've removed half of the support of the top piece across the doorway. At this point, nail it solidly in place so that it will be secure even without the side support. You may have to insert a piece of 2″ x 4″ behind it, and hold it in place with 5-minute epoxy, but at all costs you must have this part secure.

It's important to understand that all you really need to have movable is the length of wood with the striker plate in it, the part facing the door. The two pieces of molding on either side should remain in place. If they're nailed to the main upright, pry them apart and discard the nails.

Once you have the wood away from the side of the doorway, you can examine the interior of the wall. This will reveal a narrow compartment that extends until the next stud. This might be a couple of inches away or a foot or more. You must be careful not to be too ambitious. Cutting through the stud completely will weaken the wall unacceptably, and the sagging will probably ruin the fit of your secret access hatch. You can drill some compartments to hold your valuables. If your need is to conceal many small objects, such as cartridges, drill many one inch holes in the stud. You can pass lengths of plastic tubing through these into the section of wall beyond. Each length of tubing holds many cartridges, the number depending on the length and the caliber. Once you've decided on what to store and how to store it, your task is closing the compartment and making it invisible.

The best way to hold the jamb upright in place is with friction snaps. These are more secure than Velcro because they allow no play if you install them correctly. They also have much more lateral shear strength than Velcro. Be sure to use enough snaps. A couple of locator pins going into the upright and the stud will help greatly, because the piece of wood you're replacing must he able to withstand the door being slammed without coming loose. You can improvise locator pins from thick nails. If you have some drill rods, that's much better.

Installing locator pins can be fairly easy, if you know how. There are two methods useful in this case.

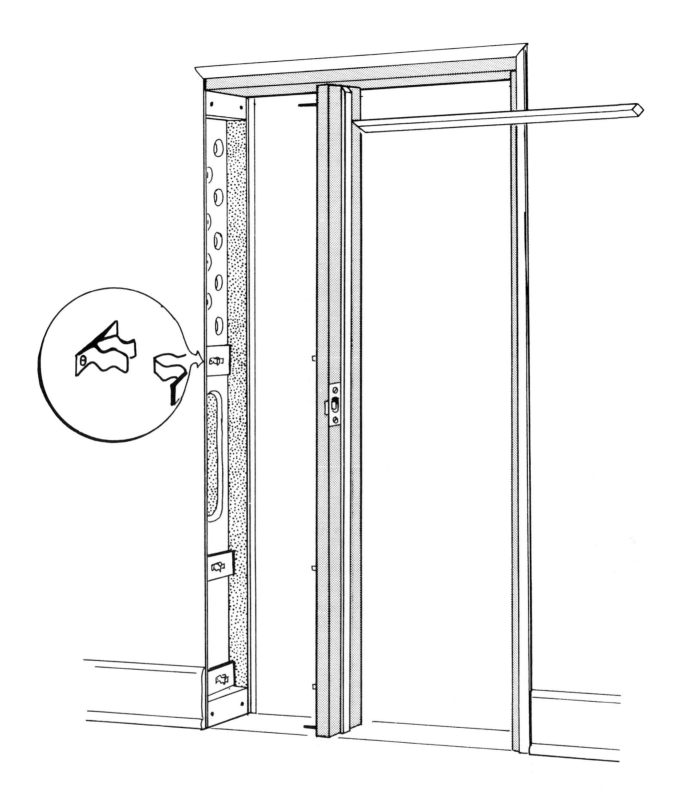

The first is to mount your secret hatch in place using the friction snaps, then drill holes through it so that pins pushed through the holes will come to rest in holes in a solid structure. If the stud is near, this will do. If not, nail a couple of pieces of 2″ x 4″ at the top and bottom of the compartment to take the locator pins. The drill size you use should be the same diameter as the pins. The odds are that you'll be using nails about four inches long for this task, and finding a drill size to match is not difficult.

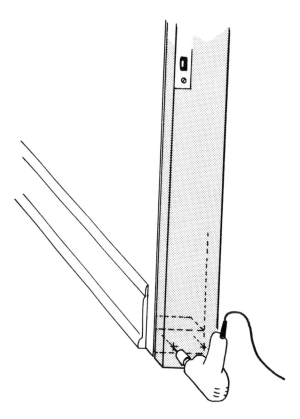

Use drill upside down in tight spot!

The second method is slightly trickier, but still workable. Decide where your locator pins are to be, and drive long nails into and through the upright from the outward side, but not while it's in place in the door frame. Use epoxy to assure that once the nails are in place, they'll stay. Use a punch to drive the nail heads below the level of the wood surface, then fill the cavities with wood putty. Let both the wood putty and the epoxy set for twenty four hours. Gently place the upright in place and press it in hard enough for the nail points to make slight indentations. Drill into these indentations. This will give you the holes for the locator pins. At the end of the job, you'll have to cover your work with paint, for sure.

Use the striker plate hole to pull the jamb away from the rest of the frame. This avoids the need for any secret handles, another complication.

Reassemble the woodwork. Nail everything back in place except, of course, for the nails holding the jamb upright. Check the cracks to make sure everything's aligned correctly.

Now look at the place at the top of the door frame where the stop molding goes. A couple of friction snaps will hold it in place. Fitting it in might be a slight problem, but some sanding should ease the way. Miter it slightly if necessary. This piece of wood is critical, because once in place, it keeps anyone from opening your secret cache.

Check for operation. Your secret door should work fairly easily without being sloppy. If too tight, miter slightly with sandpaper. Give the whole job a final once-over. You might need a coat of paint to disguise traces of your work. be discreet with the paint. You don't want a heavy coat that will leave jagged and awkward cracks where two edges meet in your secret hatchway.

CLOSETS

Closets offer several opportunities. One is the false ceiling. If you have a small closet, cut a piece of wood the exact dimensions of the interior of the closet. Nail furring strips around the inside of the closet to form a frame on three sides. This frame around the edge will hold the female parts of the friction snaps to hold the false ceiling in place. Note that the two arms will not extend completely across. This is essential to opening the secret compartment without having a protruding handle. To open, you push up on the unsupported side. This breaks the friction snaps free on the other side, which comes down. You then insert a finger and pull it the rest of the way down.

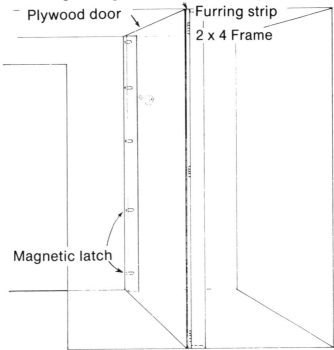

The friction snaps will not hold much of a load. Therefore, you can't use the false ceiling as a shelf. Build one or more shelves to hold your goods.

A variation on a theme is to panel the inside of the closet in cedar.[3] This is logical, because some people like cedar paneling in clothes closets for the odor. False walls, whatever their construction, can easily pass for real ones, because they all sound hollow when tapped. This is especially true in modern construction.

Many closets, especially in bedrooms, are much wider than the door. If your closet is wide, but not very deep, you have space at each side to build a false wall and a secret compartment. For this, you need to nail in a 2″ x 4″ frame, to hold the hinges and magnetic latch. A section of ¼″ plywood, painted to match the interior of the closet's paint job, serves as the door. You'll want to nail a section of furring strip down each side of your panel, because ½″ plywood isn't thick enough to allow for the screws to hold the hinges and latch. If space is at a premium, and you can't afford the one inch thickness of the furring strips, use epoxy for the job. If properly applied, epoxy will hold better than the two or three screws the hinge accommodates.

One critically important point is to avoid making any of these modifications in closets which have light fixtures inside. Part of the disguise is the gloom of a dimly lit closet, which makes detection of seams and false walls more difficult.

Many walk-in closets have light fixtures in the ceiling as well as enough room to provide a hidden compartment. If you decide to use such a closet, remove the light fixture first. Also remove the switch,

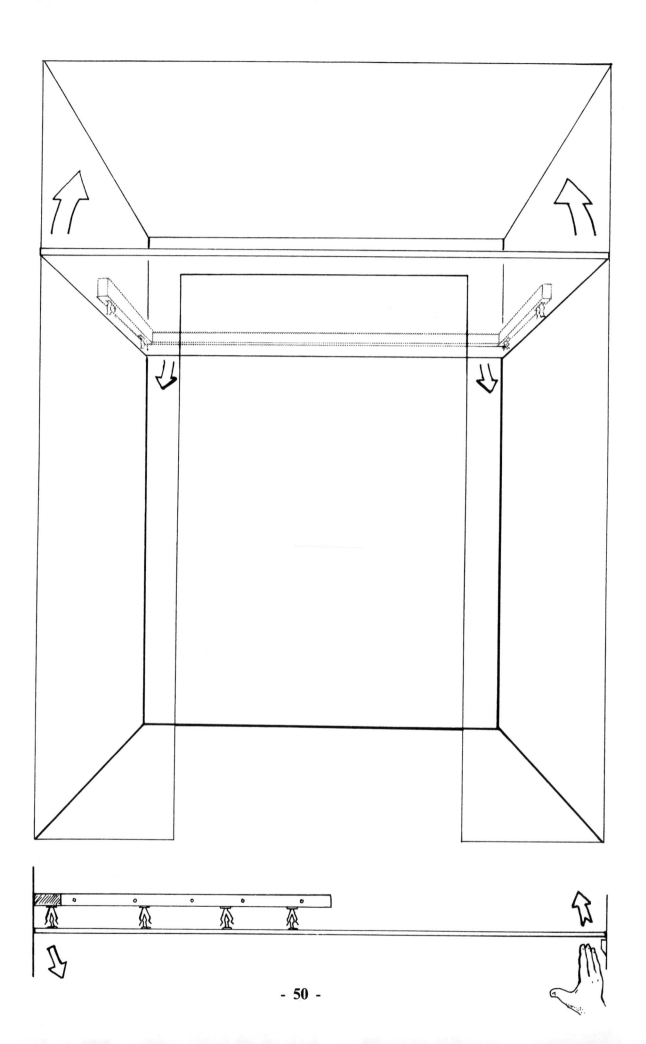

because a light switch that doesn't seem to turn on any lights will attract attention. You'll have to cover the hole in the ceiling, but you'll need to repaint the closet, anyway. In repainting, avoid the usual closet white. Use a deep off-white or a light gray to intensify the gloom.

MEDICINE CHESTS

Some medicine chests are sunk into the wall. Others are held on with screws driven into the studs. Either way, they cover a couple of square feet. If your medicine chest is sunk into the wall, you have an opening already cut into the wall, and the space under the medicine chest down to the floor is available for secret storage.[4]

If your medicine chest is hung on, you'll have to remove it and cut an access hole yourself. Usually, these medicine chests are held by screws passing through keyhole-shaped holes. These have the narrow sections at the top. This allows you to loosen the screws half a turn and lift off the cabinet. A masonry bit will drill a hole in the sheet rock to give you a start at cutting with a keyhole saw. If you don't have a keyhole saw or a masonry bit, cut a rectangular section out with a utility knife. You'll have to make several passes to cut deeply enough.

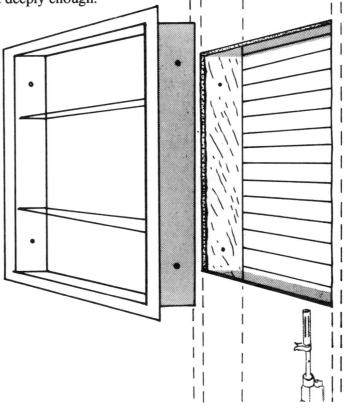

KITCHENS, UTILITY ROOMS, AND BATHROOM CABINETS

Cabinets have a lot of dead space where they meet either the floors or ceilings. Whether they contain drawers or bins, their storage spaces don't extend up to the ceiling or down to the floor. Often, the kickboards are recessed underneath, which gives an especially good opportunity to construct a hidden compartment.

Cutting away a section of a kickboard and hinging it gives access to a hidden compartment the whole length of the cabinet. This serves as burglar protection for rifles and shotguns. The installation shown is crude, and the owner depends heavily on the poor light and the shadows cast to hide it. To help, he's painted it black. This helps to dull the exterior hinges.

A more elegant installation would have resulted by using invisible hinges. There are several types made, and one commonly available brand is Soss.

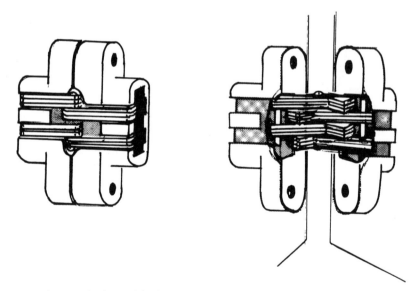

Another way to stash goods in a kitchen or bathroom cabinet is to have the entire front panel removable, and held in place with Velcro pads.[5] This is simple because it requires practically no skilled carpentry.

Bookcases also have kickboards. This design feature provides several inches of invisible space below the lowest shelf. To use the hidden space on the bottom of a bookcase, you must decide whether you're after long-term or short-term storage. If you've got some bars of precious metal, or other valuables that you're not going to need for years, and which won't be too vulnerable to fire damage, think of simply laying them on the floor underneath the bookcase when you first move it into the room. The advantage that this offers is that there's no secret door to build or to discover. Anyone who wants to search for your valuables will have to remove the books from the shelves first, then lift and remove the bookcase.

If you're worried about a half-hearted police search, this may be an advantage. If, on the other hand, you're worried about burglars ripping you off while you're away on vacation, this won't help if one of them gets the idea that you might have something in the space underneath.

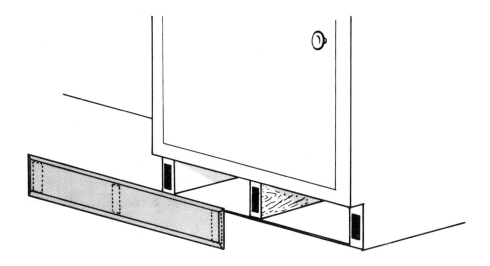

If you're planning to install secret spots in your bookcases, consider buying the build-yourself variety. There are several excellent brands out now, and they go together easily enough to make them attractive. They're not expensive, and will appeal to all but the snobs who settle for nothing less than John Stuart furniture. The main attraction is that as you assemble them, you can install hiding places.

As an option, you can hinge the kickboard instead of nailing or pinning it as the instructions direct. This is where having the bookcase on carpet helps. The thickness and resilience of the pile gives you the play to insert a thin blade to get purchase on the hinged panel when you want to open it.

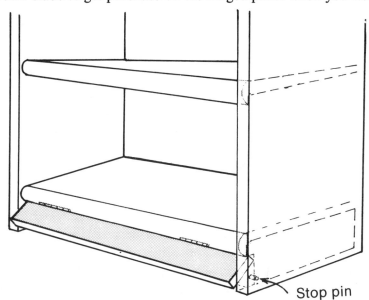

Stop pin

Counter tops offer an opportunity to hide small objects. You can use channel trim[6] to cover the cavity. Another choice is to use the existing veneer edge trim.[7] Soften the adhesive, or use a razor knife to cut it free. Drill and chisel out a cavity to hold your material, then cement the trim back into place.

The problem here is that it will be a semi-permanent installation, and gaining access to your goods will not be as quick and easy as with other hides.

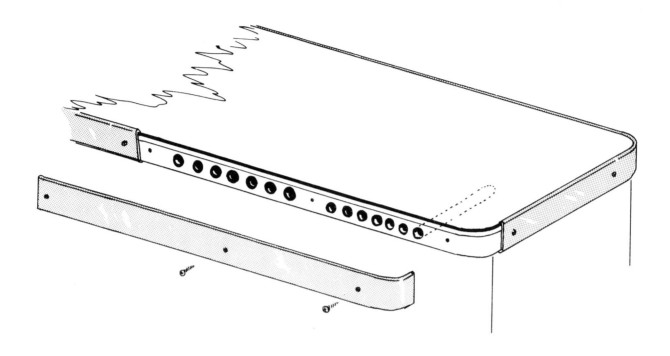

WOOD PANELING

Wood paneling in a room provides a perfect opportunity to construct a variety of hides. A modest project is a simple secret compartment in the wall behind a removable section.[8] A more ambitious one is to wall off a section of the room to yield a larger secret compartment. If there are no windows in the walled off section, it can be several feet deep without being too obvious.

One important point when constructing the access to the secret room is to have the door swinging inward to the hidden space. This avoids the possibility of scraping and wear marks on floors giving you away after some use. You also don't have to worry about hidden hinges.[9]

A compromise technique that also requires wood paneling is the false corner.[10] This is a technique which has a false corner protruding from the real corner.

This usually attracts very little attention, even though it's an irregularity. The false corner might contain a chimney, plumbing, a vertical pillar, or other essential construction details. You build it by constructing two sections of wall, each sixteen inches wide, and butting them together at right angles. One will have plaster and paint, or wallpaper, to match the wall it adjoins. The other must be movable, and it will have to be a wooden panel wall. Hinges allow it to move, as shown in the illustration.

How do you hide the crack where the two sides meet? Corner molding, that's how. Almost any building supply store carries it.

One problem: This section swings out, which means that you cannot have carpeting in the room, or you risk showing tracks after a bit of use. Be satisfied with a tile floor.

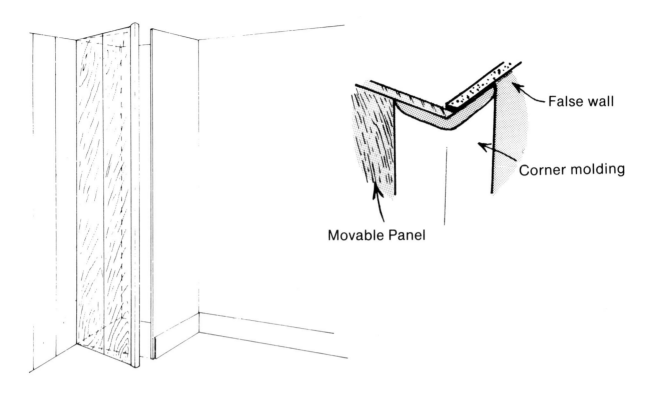

False wall

Corner molding

Movable Panel

BASEBOARDS AND MOLDING

With cheaper building techniques, the use of molding has declined in this century. The modern cracker-box tract home has none, just "sheet rock" from floor to ceiling. This isn't necessarily bad. You can install your own, fresh, without having to pry off the old stuff.

Decide on how much space you need. Be aware that often molding installed along the floor will be in front of a 2″ x 4″ used as framing. This will limit the amount of space you have available behind it.

The area along the ceiling is more likely to be open. Few modern houses are constructed with molding along the tops of interior walls, but this leaves you free to install any kind you wish. Cut into the wall, and once you have your hidden shelves in place, cover the access holes with molding. You can nail the molding in around the rest of the perimeter, but the section covering your hiding place goes on with friction snaps or Velcro.[11]

THE MIRROR STASH

You can open a large access hole in a wall and cover it with a mirror. A full-length mirror gives you convenient access to a large compartment at least sixteen inches wide.[12]

The beauty of this scheme is that you don't have to be very skilled, and there's no precise fitting of closely matching parts. A full length mirror usually fastens with brackets, each held on with one screw. To make it more convenient, and to hold the weight of the mirror adequately, make sure that your mirror's wide enough so that you can drive each screw into a wall stud.

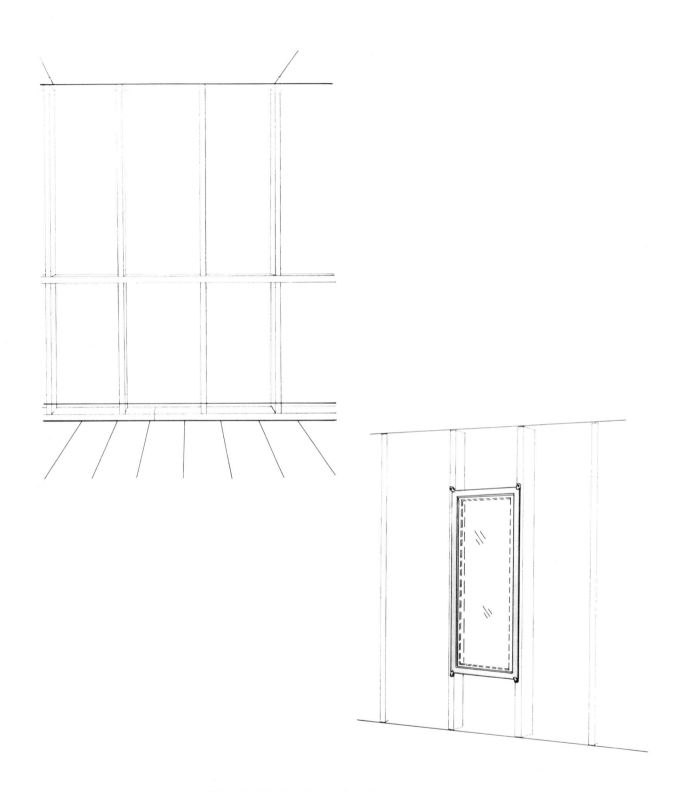

COAT OR HAT RACK STASH

This is a fairly simple method of making a medium-size stash that will be hidden behind a conventional object. A coat or hat rack covers a hole in the wall. You cut a hole in the wall and select a piece of wood plank somewhat larger to cover it and serve as a base for the coat rack.[13]

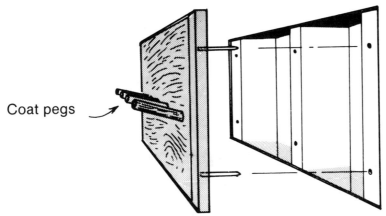

Coat pegs

Note some important construction details. To locate the rack properly on the wall, you need metal locator pins. You install them in basically the same way as you do for the door jamb pins if you intend to paint the rack. If you intend to have a natural wood finish, you have to install these more carefully.

For this you need a drill press, because you want the holes in the rack to be a precise depth, not all the way through. First, drill the holes for the pegs, don't insert them yet. Next, drill holes exactly the diameter of the locator pins, and the proper distance apart, no more than halfway into the wood. The pins should be good quality metal. The exact material doesn't matter, as long as the pins are straight and come to a point.

Apply a coat of epoxy inside each hole and press the pins in. Allow to set for at least twenty four hours. When the pins are solidly set, place the rack over the wall with the pins touching the studs where you plan to drill the mounting holes. Give the rack a sharp rap with a rubber mallet over each pin, to make the impression in the studs. This gives you a center punch for each hole you'll drill.

Drill your holes and check for fit. If you've done it properly, the pins will fit without wobbling. If the fit isn't good, plug the holes with wood putty and try again after it sets. If the fit's good, press the wooden pegs into position on the face side of the rack, using a very discreet amount of wood glue if necessary. Finish with varnish as required.

NOTES

1. *How To Hide Anything,* Michael Connor, (Boulder, Colorado, Paladin Press, 1984) pp. 14-15.

2. *How To Hide Almost Anything,* David Krotz, (New York, William Morrow and Company, 1975) pp. 36-40.

3. *Ibid.,* p. 97.

4. *Secret Hiding Places,* Charles Robinson, (Cornville, Arizona, Desert Publications, 1981) pp. 31-32.

5. *How To Hide Anything,* p. 12.

6. *Secret Hiding Places,* pp. 25-26.

7. *How To Hide Anything,* pp. 39-40.

8. *Hidden Riches,* Chas. M. Albano, (Tacoma, Washington, Erco, Inc., 1974) p. 51.

9. *Secret Hiding Places,* p. 51.

10. *How To Hide Almost Anything,* pp. 93-95.

11. *Secret Hiding Places,* p. 37.

12. *Ibid.,* p. 28-29.

13. *Ibid.,* pp. 39-41.

HIDING PLACES IN THE HOME:
STRUCTURES AND COMPARTMENTS
PART III

STAIRWAYS

Traditional staircases have "dead space" underneath, and in some instances the design of the structure puts this dead space to use. There may be a closet or understairs storage. Typically, a flight of stairs continues under the descender from the floor above. This means that the staircase can only have a closet under it at the bottom story.

If the staircase is enclosed, there may be some useful space for small objects behind the risers. You'll find almost a foot of space between the stairs you see and the ceiling for the section of stair below.

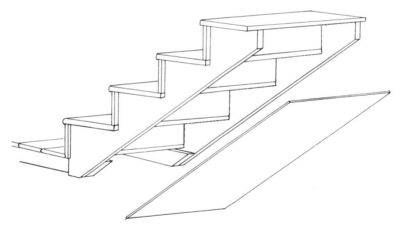

The first step is to remove the riser. This can be difficult, if the risers and treads are routed out. Sometimes, they're set into the wall on one side and the stringer on the other.[1] There may be wedges to hold the treads and risers without nails, and if the risers are let into the above tread and routed for the tread below, they'll be very difficult to dismantle.

The basic technique is to hinge the riser so that it moves back under pressure to reveal the hidden compartment behind it. A set of hinges along the upper edge of the riser will allow it to swing.[2]

A complication is carpeting. This requires more work, but has the advantage of covering up butchered carpentry. Frankly, disassembling a staircase can be butchery, and there might be some prying to do with a crowbar. This inevitably leaves marks, and carpeting will help cover the traces.[3]

Having separate panels of carpeting on each riser and tread will allow this. It's not hard to match panels of carpet to make them seem one piece, but, if there's any doubt, using two different shades of the same color can help cover any discrepancies. Having the treads dark blue, and the risers a lighter blue is one combination.

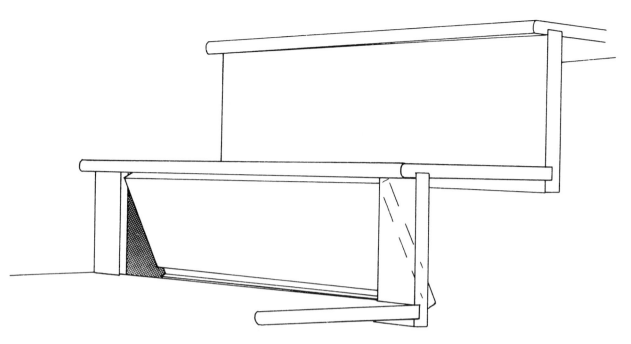

Another possibility is present if the stairway has a cased free side.[4] This offers a ready made storage compartment within the case. The railing on top can serve as a lid, either hinged or set into friction snaps.

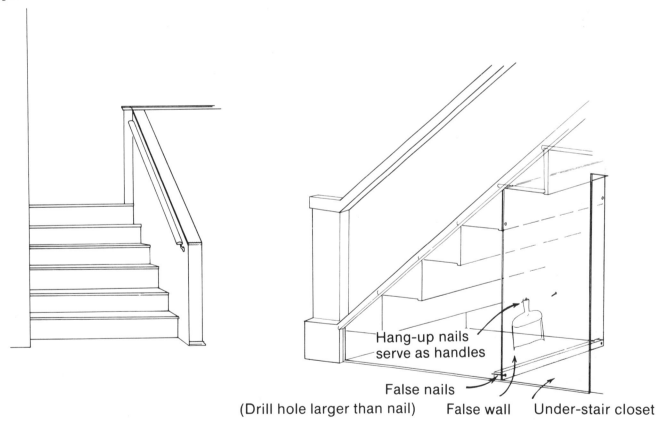

Hang-up nails
serve as handles

False nails
(Drill hole larger than nail)   False wall   Under-stair closet

Using the space under the bottom flight of stairs is an unimaginative possibility. Although this has received a lot of attention,[5] only the dullest searcher would overlook it.

SHELVES

An ingenious way of creating a secret compartment within a wall and hiding the seams of the trap doors is to conceal it with on-the-wall shelving.[6] A removable section of the shelving hides the lines of the trap door, which is swung in the usual manner.

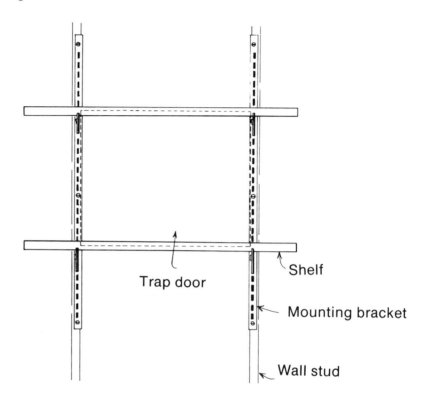

Trap door

Shelf

Mounting bracket

Wall stud

UNDER THE FLOORBOARDS AND UNDERGROUND

This method has its value, but it's limited. People have hidden all sorts of contraband under the floorboards, even dead bodies.[7]

It requires very careful work, and the ideal under-the-floor hiding place is open to question. One opinion is to avoid placing anything under the floorboards at the edge of a room, because simply lifting a section of the carpet will easily disclose it.[8]

This is good reasoning, but there are other considerations. One is how solid the lid of the hide is. It's revealing to have a floorboard squeak, and worse for one to cave in. People are more likely to walk in the center of a room than along the walls.

One solution is to have the hide protected by a piece of furniture, to dissuade a casual search. Nothing will deter a professional and determined searcher. A bureau, located logically along a wall, can easily cover a hiding place, and hold down a section of the room's carpet.

In constructing a floorboard hide, it's important to consider whether your floor is the ceiling of a floor below you. If you're not on the bottom floor or basement, it is. This limits the weight of the material you can hide. You can hide some documents, a few rolls of film, and perhaps a few kilos of dope, but if you try to conceal a thousand rounds of 5.56 ammo you're likely to cause a slight cave-in.

There are exceptions in industrial buildings, but residences are typically constructed as cheaply as possible, just strongly enough to meet the building code, and the ceilings are cheap indeed. If you're near houses under construction, take a walk over to inspect them. Look at the ceiling fixtures, and note how they're all attached to beams, not simply set into the drywall. Also note how the drywall is attached. You'll see the same nails used to fasten wall sections. This combination doesn't have much strength, and if you plan to store anything heavy in a floor that's also the ceiling of the floor below, plan to have brackets to hold your material.

It's much easier to hide the access panel if the nature of the floor allows it. Carpeting is only a superficial hide, but a parquet floor or vinyl tiles produce a pattern of seams that effectively hide the outline of the panel.

This brings up the possibility of a secret room underground. If you have a ground floor with parquet or tile, you can excavate and construct a complete hidden room with a good chance of total concealment from all but the most exhaustive search.

The big problem with secret rooms is that the inside and outside dimensions don't add up. It's very easy to discover a secret room by using a tape measure. The discrepancy will be immediately obvious, and in a small house or apartment, will be so glaring that a searcher will spot it by eye. No amount of careful work or craftsmanship will hide it effectively.

The situation is different when building underground. The problem is only to conceal the entrance adequately. Cosmetic concealment is easy when the floor is tiles. This is the easiest method, because of low cost compared to parquet. The second aspect of concealment is to avoid a hollow sound when someone walks on that section of floor. Solid construction will help here.

The trap door will have to be substantial, but an extra layer of expanded styrofoam insulation will deaden further any possible hollow sound.

Don't think, however, that constructing an underground room is just a matter of digging up the floor and excavating until you've got it large enough. If you're using a cottage in the country, you'll probably not have any pipes or electrical conduits underground, and it pays to get a copy of the building plans before starting out.

If you can't get the plans, you'll have to take your chances. You might have a large drain pipe in the center of your hidden room, but if you can live with this, and work around it, you'll be successful. The most important point to watch is to use only hand tools when excavating, and to be careful. Penetrating a water pipe will flood your room, and you might not be able to repair the break. If this happens, and you have to call the water company, your secret's gone. Hitting an electrical conduit can be worse, as you can understand.

Disposing of the dirt and debris is a problem. If you want your hide to be truly secret, you must construct it in secret. You can easily have to dispose of several tons of material from the excavation, and this means that you'll have to have this planned out before you begin.

Disposal can easily take a long time. If you plan to carry it out a shopping-bag-full at a time, and drop it off in public garbage cans, you'll have quite a project on your hands. You can, as an alternative, simply displace the dirt on your property. If you like gardening, construct planter boxes and use your dirt to fill them, rather than purchasing top soil.

You may also want to construct an underground hide outside in the garden. The same problems apply, but with one more hazard. Is anyone going to see or hear you building it? The prospect of digging it out at night isn't attractive. Sounds also carry at night. This problem may be insoluble.

However, if you're normally seen working in the garden, and your neighbors aren't too nosy, you might be able to do it. A high fence or wall will help, but only if the houses in your area are normally built this way.

There are basically two methods of excavation. One is tunneling. This is digging an access hole vertically and then striking out horizontally for the main work. This will do if you're digging a tunnel or an underground bowling alley, but for your most likely purpose, you'll want to "cut and cover."

This means digging a pit the size of the underground room, then constructing the roof. This is the most practical method to use, even indoors, unless there's a priceless parquet floor you must disturb as little as possible.

Constructing your roof at the end lets you provide maximum strength, without risk of collapse halfway through. The roof will be very important, both for strength and to avoid any hollow sounds.

One problem is shoring. This means bracing your walls as you dig. There are a number of ways to do this, some of them very elaborate. A lot depends on your purpose. If you're constructing a bomb shelter, you'll want very solid construction, and reinforced concrete isn't too much. If you're building just a small space to conceal some material or one or two people for a short time, you can use simpler methods.

If you want to take it a step further, you can use your wood shoring as a mold for pouring concrete. This is more involved. As a rough guide, you can expect to use a ton of concrete to line an 8′ x 10′ underground room.

As you dig, save any rocks you find. These will serve to line a sump. Depending on where you live, you'll have a problem with water. In areas of heavy rainfall, you'll need a lot of drainage. The quality of drainage you get will depend on the size of your sump and also on the soil. Clay soil doesn't absorb well.

In some instances, a pole driven into the ground at one corner of your underground room will serve to create an adequate drain.[9]

Hiding the access hatch is the final problem, and the solution is fairly simple in principle. Blend it in with the surroundings. Trying to build a hatch in the middle of a lawn will never work because the seam will show. You may also have a problem with the level of the hatch not matching the surrounding grass.

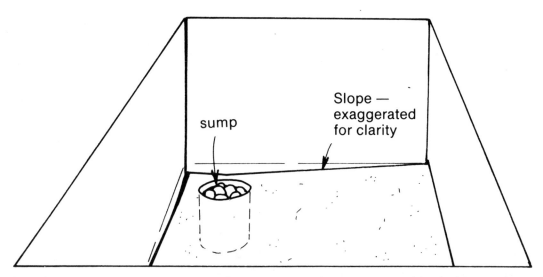

Lay tile on your lawn. A patch of tile with an umbrella to one side and some lawn furniture surrounding it will look in place and appropriate. Another way is to construct a cement walkway. Have each slab separate from the rest, to create a distinct seam between the slabs. One of them, of course, will be your access hatch.

A quick and dirty expedient for hiding an access hatch is an above ground pool. This gives an instant cover, and will discourage a superficial searcher, but it's troublesome to gain access. You have to drain the water, which can take hours. It also takes hours to refill. Another problem is the weight. Before using this method, calculate how much water will be on the roof of your underground room.

Water weighs about 62 lbs per cubic foot for fresh water. If your room is 8' x 10' and the roof is totally covered with a pool, and the watear is four feet deep, that's 8 x 10 x 4 cubic feet of water. That's 320 cubic feet, and at 62 lbs per cubic foot, a total of 19,840 lbs. That's almost ten tons. Can your structure hold that?

Thus, we see that an underground room can have certain problems as well as certain advantages. It's a lot of work, and before you start such an ambitious project, be sure that you'll need it.

Closely allied to underground rooms is burial of small objects. There are a couple of problems with burial apart from adequately waterproofing your material. You can easily handle waterproofing by using plastic pipe, which is inexpensive and commonly available.

One problem is disguising your hide. If you need quick access and have to get into it fairly often, use a flower bed. With freshly dug soil, this will hide your excavation.

Another problem is security. The best way to hide something underground against a determined search is to enlarge the potential search area beyond practical possibility. What this means, in plain language, is to bury it as far away from your home as is practical. A searcher may go over your yard with a metal detector, but he can't go over every inch of the twenty mile circle around your home.

If you must bury something metallic in your yard, try to bury it under a pipe or electrical conduit. This will confuse anyone with a metal detector. It's also an obvious trick, and you might be better off throwing a few pieces of scrap iron and steel around in your yard. Bolts and nuts buried close to the surface will give as intense a reading as larger objects buried deeply, and with enough of these false echoes, a searcher will either have to dig up your entire yard or give up.

FALSE CHIMNEYS

One fairly ingenious way of constructing a medium-sized stash in a private house is to build a false chimney.[10] False fireplaces and chimneys are common construction features in houses, and don't attract undue attention. Having a totally false inoperative chimney means that you can have the whole space for your stash, and not have to shoehorn it in between the chimney pipe and the outer casing.

SEMI-STRUCTURAL HIDES

Most residences have permanent and semi-permanent fittings and accessories that serves as hides. Look at the fence around your house. Are the fence posts wood or are they metal tubes? If they're wood, drilling them out to make cavities for concealment will be a bit of work, but if they're metal tubes, you have some ready made hiding places. Remove the cap of each vertical to expose the hide.[11]

Drainpipes are ready made hides. A slim object on the end of a string and attached with a hook, will fit in a drainpipe. The only problem comes from the drainpipe's function. Your contraband must be invulnerable to water damage or be thoroughly waterproofed.

Refrigerators and freezers have easily removable inside panels. You can unscrew these and store small objects in the insulation.

Kitchen stoves also have dead space and access panels which aren't always immediately obvious. Of course, you don't want to store anything in the oven's cavity, unless it's absolutely invulnerable to heat damage. If your stove's a fancy modern model, with a timer and an elaborate control panel, you'll usually find that the space behind the panel offers a hide.

The problem with structural and semi-structural hides is that they're not readily portable. For convenience, you may want to hide material in objects you can carry easily. We'll consider these next.

NOTES

1. *House Construction Details,* Nelson Burbank and Herbert Pfister, (New York, Simmons-Boardman Publishing Corp., 1968) p. 213.

2. *Secret Hiding Places,* Charles Robinson, (Cornville, Arizona, Desert Publications, 1981) pp. 42-43.

3. *How To Hide Almost Anything,* David Krotz, (New York, William Morrow and Company, 1975) pp. 70-73.

4. *House Construction Details,* p. 217.

5. *How To Hide Anything,* Michael Connor, (Boulder, Colorado, Paladin Press, 1984) pp. 16-17, and *Secret Hiding Places*, pp. 54-55.

6. *Secret Hiding Places,* pp. 44-45.

7. *Ten Rillington Place,* Ludovic Kennedy (New York, Simon & Schuster, 1961). This is the fascinating story of John Christie, the London-based serial murderer of the 1940s and 1950s. He disposed of several female associates, including his wife. His wife and another went under the floorboards in his living room. A couple of others went into a false wall in his kitchen. More were buried in his back yard. Strangely, one of his tenants was arrested and convicted of two of Christie's murders and was hanged for them. Christie got his a couple of years later, when he was arrested, tried, and executed.

Hiding bodies in walls is not a new practice, and an almost obsolete French verb, "enmurer," refers to putting corpses in walls. Literally translated, it means "to wall up" but it refers to emplacing bodies, not just constructing a wall. It dates from medieval times, when walls were stone, not sheetrock, and the odor of decomposition might be less noticeable because of the thickness of the masonry. Dukes and counts got rid of wives this way.

8. *How To Hide Anything,* p. 20.

9. *Ibid.,* p. 71.

10. *Ibid.,* p. 34.

11. *Ibid.,* p. 33.

MISCELLANEOUS HIDING PLACES IN THE HOME

There are a number of odd hiding places that are readily available, easy to place into service, and sometimes even offer the additional advantage of portability. This may outweigh what they lack in security.

SHOWER CURTAIN RODS

These are always hollow metal tubes. Some of these are screwed into the wall. Others held by spring pressure are easy to take down and disassemble. All will hold small items such as gems and rounds of ammunition. They'll also hold rolled up papers, such as documents and money.[1]

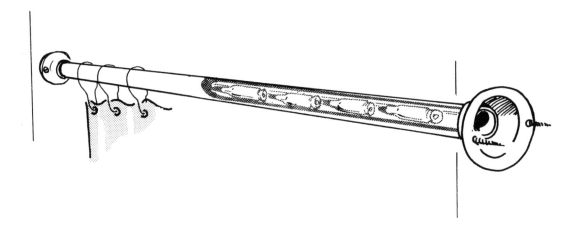

CONVENTIONAL CURTAIN RODS

Curtain rods come in all types. Most are metal. Some are wood. Some are metal finished to look like wood. The metal ones are hollow. Most have end caps. The caps simply are slide fits, and are easy to remove for access.[2]

KITCHEN AND UTILITY ROOM

Food and detergent containers are natural hiding places. They're very accessible, which means that security is slight, but for quick and dirty hiding places with a minimum of trouble, they'll do fine.

One place to start is the freezer. Wrapping small items in waxed paper, supermarket paper, or aluminum foil prepares them for an inconspicuous existence in the freezer. A superficial search will disclose them, though. One way to gain some extra security is to lay an extra wrapping of ground beef around your material before freezing. A searcher who unwraps the aluminum foil will see only the ground beef and if he stops there, you're safe. If he has a metal detector, and your stash contains metal, you're in trouble.

One place to hide metal objects is in metal cans.[3] Soak the label off with water, then cut the can across its diameter with a hacksaw. Empty the can out and set the contents aside if you want to repack them. Fabricate an insert from thin metal. This insert serves as a liner to hold the two parts of the can together.

Thin metal insert

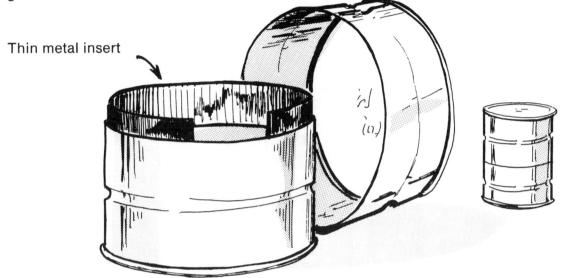

How bulky is what you need to hide? If it's small, such as a jewel, you can mix it with the can's contents and this will provide an extra disguise if anyone opens the can. If it's vulnerable to moisture damage, and you can't waterproof it, you'll have to fill the space with something else. Whatever your filler may be, make sure it doesn't rattle and make sure the can weighs approximately the same as originally.

You can hold the insert in place with solder or super glue. If you want it to hold well, be sure the metal is dry before using solder or glue. Replace the label.

Cereal and detergent boxes are useful stashes, especially for paper and other non-metallic objects. The strategy is to undo them from the bottom. Use an X-Acto knife or utility knife, and cut through the layer of glue rather than the cardboard. Most of these boxes have a paper or plastic liner to hold the contents. Usually, the liner is glued to the inside of the box. If it isn't, glue it. This will give you an extra barrier in case of a search. A searcher who opens the box from the top and pours out the contents may stop there, unless your contraband is so heavy that he can feel that it's not an empty box by its heft. Use Elmer's glue to reseal the box.[4]

Don't bother to hide anything in the cut out pages of a book. This will only work if the searcher doesn't even pick up the book. However, if he does, and he merely riffles the pages, anything hidden in a cut out will show.

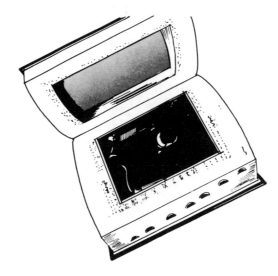

A small object, such as a strip of microfilm, will slide down the spine of a hardback book. Wrap it in plastic first, and hold it in place with a drop of glue.

A quick and dirty hiding place is in the garbage, especially if you have the stale remains of a meal sitting on top of your contraband. The psychological deterrent will stop some searchers. Another, similarly unattractive hiding place is in a cat box. Burying contraband in kitty litter will conceal it, but note that your cat may uncover it while using his sandbox.

OTHER HOLLOW OBJECTS

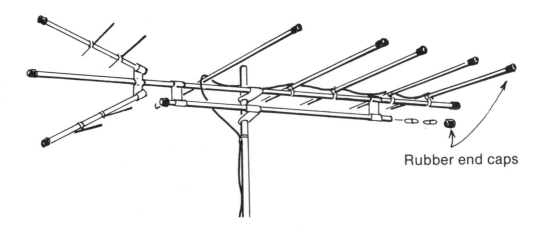

Rubber end caps

The tubes of a TV antenna will conceal some small objects. Space is limited, but if you have the antenna mounted on the roof, any searcher will be greatly inconvenienced. So will you, if you have to get at your stash often.[5]

Many household and garden tools have hollow metal or plastic handles. Most have convenient end caps, easy to remove for quick access. Some tools, such as shovels, have wooden handles. These are fairly easy to drill out for a short way, enough to conceal small objects. Remove the tool head and ferrule, drill, insert your material, and replace the tool head.[6] Some tool heads screw on. These offer the fewest problems. One that attaches with a pin or dowel will require you to drill the hole extra deeply to clear the pin. A tool head that's a press fit can cause problems. These are cheap, and usually come loose quickly. For security, hold it on with a shot of glue.

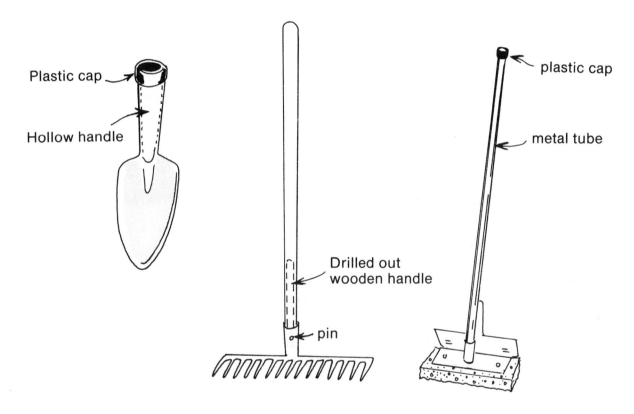

Plastic cap

Hollow handle

Drilled out
wooden handle

pin

plastic cap

metal tube

BATHROOM ITEMS

A cesspool offers the same sort of psychological security as the above mentioned catbox, but not everyone has a cesspool. A quick indoor counterpart to this is an inoperative toilet. If you have more than one toilet, disable one by removing the connecting rod, and breaking it off. Use the toilet several times, copiously, fecal matter being a strong psychological barrier to a search. Drop your material in, weighting it if necessary to make it sink to the bottom. Make sure it's in an impervious wrapper.

For retrieval, you'll want to keep a pair of rubber gloves on hand in another room, so that no searcher will make the connection. If you don't have gloves, you should have a strong stomach.

A metal toothpaste tube makes an excellent hide.[7] Some are now made of plastic, and these are less convenient for hiding small items. Resealing them requires heat, because they won't hold a fold as will one made of tin. Don't be deterred by the tin tube's being sealed. Unroll it and cut off the end. Push your material into the toothpaste and fold up the end once more.

If you need more space, squeeze the toothpaste out into a confectioner's icing bag and stash your material in the toothpaste tube. Squeeze enough toothpaste to fill the remaining space in the tube, and close it by folding, as described before.

A jar of cold cream is excellent for hiding things. Push your material to the bottom, and screw the jar shut. A can of shoe polish is almost as useful, but it's smaller. You need to melt the shoe polish to cast around the material you're concealing, to give an untampered look to it.

If you have to hide something in a hurry, dropping it into the bottom of the bathroom wastebasket can give some protection if there's a fresh, used sanitary pad on top. The psychological deterrent again.

SEX TOYS

The psychological deterrent to search is very important, and one way to make it work for you is to use a distraction. Get some sex toys, the kinkier the better, and hide your material inside them. They can be just as good hides as other objects, but someone searching your home will be thinking about exactly what turns you on, instead of keeping his mind on his job.

This can be exceptionally valuable when trying to pass something through customs, because you can use your apparent embarrassment to distract customs officers. It will also work during a warrant search or a surreptitious "toss" of your living quarters. Even without your being present, sexual goods provide searching officers an opportunity for a laugh at your expense, at the same time taking their minds off their job.

Let's say that you're hiding diamonds, and you have them rolled up inside "lambskin" contraceptives. One brand of these (Fourex) comes in plastic capsules which you can open and reseal. A piece of blue tape holds the two halves together. Having a vibrator and a few other toys will distract the customs guard, as you cringe with the exposure of these embarrassing items in your luggage.

Many of these sex toys have cavities. An artificial penis, or a male masturbation device is likely to have a space for hiding small things. Some electrically operated ones have battery compartments.

A short stack of homosexual magazines will provoke a lot of snickers at your expense. If they were girlie magazines, officers would look at them carefully, but will give homosexual and other perverted publications only a superficial look. If there are some documents between the pages that are stuck together, they won't see them.

The more bizarre, the better. If you have some sado-masochistic magazines, officers probably won't inspect the high fur boots for hollow heels, and may not even think that the handles of your whips are hollow.

The only caution is an obvious one. Don't take any of these items into a country where they're illegal. Don't have them in your possession in such a country.

TAPE CASSETTES

There are basically two kinds of tape cassettes: the good quality ones that are held together with screws, and the heat sealed cheapies. Both have dead space inside for hiding material. The ones with screw heads showing invite inspection. The heat sealed ones that will be damaged by disassembly offer some protection.[8] You open them with a hot blade and reseal them with cyanoacrylate glue.

CAST ITEMS

Certain items are very good for hiding things because they look tamperproof. Chocolate bars and bars of soap are examples. Actually, they're tamperproof, but you can refabricate them.

The first step is to get some silicon rubber. General Electric or Dow RTV-20 is one type that works well. With the silicon rubber, you make a mold of the bar. Chocolate is easier to handle, because a chocolate bar has only one face and that's all you have to worry about. Once you have your mold, you melt the chocolate and recast it with your material cast into the bar.

An ingenious way of casting your own chocolate bars with minimal expense is to buy a child's rubber mold set. These are made for children to cast small statues of animals, etc., in plaster. Instead, cast them in chocolate, and wrap them in foil of various colors. Arrange them in a gift box, put a card on the box, and you have another medium-security stash.

Soap bars have two faces, and you have to make a split mold. This is a far more difficult technique, and may be beyond your skill. Some brands of soap bars, however, have visible seam lines, and you can make a mold for these.

Rewrapping a bar of soap or chocolate is usually no problem, and careful unwrapping will preserve the wrapping paper for the repackaging. A couple of drops of super glue will do the rest. A good point is that a used bar of soap will attract less suspicion than a fresh and wrapped one.[9] A few hairs and bits of crud embedded in the surface makes it unattractive to even touch.

A hairbrush or bathbrush will, if it's large enough, offer a hiding place for small objects.

CIGARETTE LIGHTERS

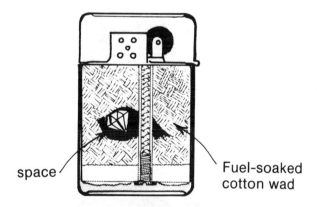

space — Fuel-soaked cotton wad

There have been instances of cigarette lighters being made into weapons, but you won't need anything that exotic. The benzene-type lighter has a removable holder where the fuel is held in a wad of cotton.[10] Prying out the cotton and inserting your material will work, especially if you're hiding gems or other material which will not be damaged by the petroleum distillate. You can even light a cigarette with the lighter this way.

The butane-type lighters won't adapt well to this treatment. While it's true that you can saw the bottom off and reattach it with a hot blade, the lighter won't work because the butane will have evaporated. Refillable butane lighters are rare today, but it's possible, with good metal working skill, to open the fuel tank, insert material, and reseal it to hold the pressurized butane. That way, the lighter will work if an inspector tries it.

PRESSURE CANS

While it's possible, with the right tools and facilities, to open and reseal pressure cans, it's usually not practical. A shaving cream can will, if handled correctly, show few signs of tampering.[11] You can pry it open and reseal it with an improvised press fabricated from pliers or tongs. The mechanical end of it is workable, but unless the contraband is liquid and looks and smells like shaving cream, anyone pressing the valve will wonder why no shaving cream comes out.

Likewise, it's possible to open a pull top soda pop can, drain the liquid, and refill it with powder or liquid that will pass through the small aperture. A drop of cyanoacrylate glue seals the can.[12] Matching the weight and feel of the original contents is difficult. Powder doesn't weigh the same, and anyone shaking the can will not hear a splash as he would with a real soda can.

CERAMICS

A ceramic object offers a very good hiding place, but there's one severe limitation. Anything made of metal will show on a metal detector. One way to outfox these, is to use a metallic glaze, but this is only partial protection. Searchers who are truly suspicious will break open the ceramic objects to resolve any doubts.

If you're truly skilled at ceramics, you can try to duplicate cups and saucers in a name brand set. It's less likely that searchers will break every piece of an obviously valuable set to find contraband, while they might not have any inhibitions about smashing a nondescript piece that has "homemade" all over it.

ELECTRONIC ITEMS

Computers, radios, TV sets, and other electronic toys and tools are so common that they're naturals for creating hides. A side effect of miniaturization is that there's a lot of "dead space" inside most of them. As a start, take the cover off one that you plan to use as a hide, and examine the leftover space.

A light piece of contraband, wrapped to muffle rattling, will fit easily. It helps if the piece of equipment is in operating condition, so don't use the battery compartment for this.

Fake label

For very flat objects, it's possible to create a space under the label. You can try prying off the label, or steaming it off, but the easiest way is to create your own. Many electronic toys and tools are made in the Orient, and have cheaply printed and badly written labels, composed by someone unfamiliar with the English language. Typing directions for use, or technical specifications, onto a square of paper, drawing a border around it, and making a photocopy of the original will make a passable label. Use awkward phrasing, such as: "Install surely batteries in proper way." Glue this on any clear area inside your unit.

It's possible to hide material inside individual components.[13] There's one important caution: Make sure that the device is still in operating condition after you've finished. One exception to this is possible only when you're concealing something in your home. You can have a broken device gathering dust in a basement or attic, or simply thrown into a garbage bag under the sink.

Otherwise, the device must work so as not to provoke the question of why not. It's possible to cut open a dry cell battery with a sharp knife, insert the stash, and reseal it with dolser or super glue, but the battery may not work or even conduct electricity after this treatment. If this is the case, carry it as a spare.

Individual electronic components can be opened and resealed. A large capacitor is usually in a can made of thin aluminum. Prying the end off, inserting the contraband, and resealing it will serve for hiding small objects. Resistors are usually made of epoxy or plastic, and it's not worth even trying to cut them open. Instead, cast your own.

Use a real resistor as a pattern, and make a mold of it. Use Brownell's "Acra-Cast" molding kit, obtainable from: Brownell's, Inc., Route 2, Box 1, Montezuma, IA 50171.

The kit costs about eleven dollars, and will make castings of almost anything.

To make your fake resistors, use pieces of scrap wire for "tails." The material to use for casting fake resistors is Brownell's "Acraglas Gel" kit, which is a nylon-filled epoxy casting kit. The advantage of this one is that it was originally designed for glass bedding wood rifle stocks, and comes with an envelope of brown dye to match the wood. By coincidence, many resistors are of brown plastic, with rings of various colors painted on to denote their values. The "Acraglas Gel" kit costs slightly more than eight dollars, and contains two ounces each of resin and hardener, enough to cast a whole bunch!

The important point is not to use these in place of any real electronic component in the device you're modifying. Solder the fake resistor into place in parallel with any other, and don't worry about it. If you've made it properly, it won't conduct any electricity, and therefore won't short out the circuit. Few searchers will be able to go over a piece of electronic equipment component by component to check that they all work the way they're supposed to.

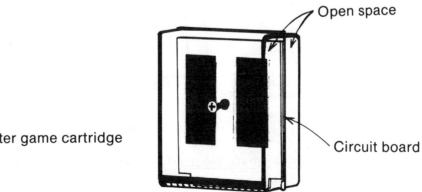

Open space

Computer game cartridge

Circuit board

Game chips for computer games are usually in small plastic housings that have a connector for plugging into the computer. Some of these are held together by a screw under the label. The label comes off with solvent or steaming, exposing the screws.

Once you have the two valves undone, you conceal your material without damaging the "guts" of the unit, making sure that no rattle betrays you. Screw the two halves together once more, reseal the label, and you're set.[14]

One important precaution to take is to buy several of these when you start concealing objects. You're bound to ruin one or two while developing your technique. Admit this from the start, and have a couple of extras on hand with which to make your mistakes.

CAMERAS

These are excellent for hiding material, but with limitations. If you're traveling, a camera's a better stash than if you're at home, because customs officers always assume that opening a traveler's camera will ruin film inside because it's loaded. If you're being searched at home, it's either by police with a warrant, or burglars without, and in either case they're likely to open the camera.

There's very little dead space inside a camera. One small hide is in the bellows under the mirror of an SLR. Another is in a roll of film.

In 35mm cameras, film comes in metal or plastic cassettes, or cartridges. The Kodak cartridges are not reusable, because the end caps are stab crimped into place. You can pry one end cap off carefully, cut a cavity in the film, and reseal it.[15]

It's easier to buy European or Japanese made film. Their cassettes have screw or bayonet end caps, or the metal type that hold with spring pressure.

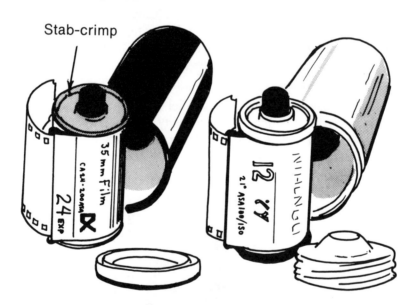

Do you use a fresh roll of film, or one that's apparently been exposed? If you use a fresh one, and have it threaded into the camera's transport system, you may be asked to crank off a frame or two. If you have a cassette in your camera bag with no tongue of film protruding, your stating that it's exposed is very credible. You can assume that no customs officer will ask you to open it.

If you're the subject of a search warrant, on the other hand, you can expect that the officers will go over everything with a fine tooth comb. The prospect of ruining a roll of film won't deter them, unless they decide to send the "exposed" film to their lab for processing in the hope of finding something incriminating on the film.

Polaroid film packs have some dead space, especially if you've run off several exposures. It's also possible to remove them from the camera and reinsert them without ruining any film if you can do it by "feel" in total darkness. The housing is made of very thin sheet steel, and it snaps apart to allow you to insert your material.

As an extra psychological deterrent, you may wish to insert the contraband in broad daylight, ruining the film. If you then find yourself being searched, you can tell the officer handling your camera that he's ruining your film, pop off an exposure, and "prove" it to him by showing him the blank film. A show of anger might divert his search at that critical moment.

NOTES

1. *How To Hide Anything,* Michael Connor, (Boulder, Colorado, Paladin Press, 1984) p. 96.

2. *Ibid.,* pp. 19-20.

3. *Secret Hiding Places,* Charles Robinson, (Cornville, Arizona, Desert Publications, 1981) pp. 20-23.

4. *Ibid.,* pp. 19-20.

5. *How to Hide Anything,* p. 21.

6. *Ibid.,* pp. 25-26.

7. *Duty Free,* Michael Connor, (Boulder, Colorado, Paladin Press, 1983) p.31.

8. *Ibid.,* pp. 39-41.

9. *Ibid.,* p. 45.

10. *Ibid.,* pp. 53-55.

11. *Ibid.,* pp. 42-44.

12. *Ibid.,* pp. 48-49.

13. *Sneak It Through,* Michael Connor, (Boulder, Colorado, Paladin Press, 1984) pp. 30-38.

14. *Ibid.,* pp. 36-37.

15. *Ibid.,* p. 25.

ON YOUR PERSON

Hiding things on your person may or may not work. There are several factors to consider, because the human body is limited in space, and hiding places are few.

Is the object metallic or non-metallic? If metallic, you'd better not carry it anywhere there are electronic search gates, unless you know for sure that the sensitivity of the gate is low. Some of the latest models, used in high security installations, will pick up a paperclip or shoelace grommet. It doesn't matter if your material is a weapon or not. If it's metallic, you don't want it detected. One way around this is to carry it in another metal object.

How large is the object? Can you hide it in a body cavity? If so, it's slightly more secure. Will it fit in an object you normally carry?

Finally, what's the penalty for getting caught? Would it be better or more secure to send your material on ahead, by mail or truck, or do you need quick access?

Let's look for hiding places on the person, starting at the top.

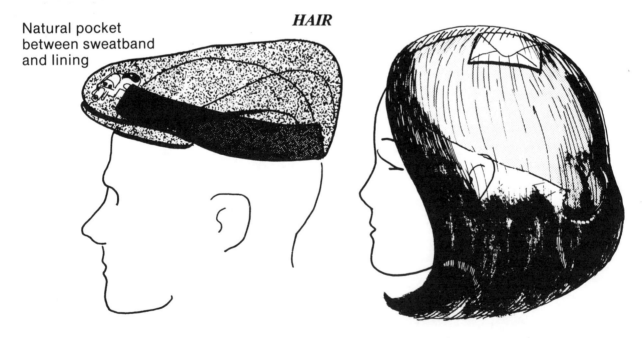

HAIR

Natural pocket between sweatband and lining

If you're bald, you can skip to the next section, unless you've decided to wear a wig or toupee. Concealing small flat objects under a hairpiece will enable evading a superficial search, but never a strip search.

If you have thick, long, or bushy hair, consider the possibility of hiding small objects in it. A hat makes a good accessory for concealing small objects. A very light and small firearm, such as a mini-revolver, will fit even under a baseball cap. Use a hat liner for small flat objects, such as microfilm, a couple of bills, or tickets.

MOUTH, EARS, AND NOSE

You can conceal something here for a short time. The mouth, the biggest cavity, can conceal the most but there's the danger of swallowing or choking on your material.

As a sidelight, some people have a hollow tooth. Heinrich Himmler, chief of the SS and the German Security Police, committed suicide shortly after capture by the British by using a pellet of cyanide he had kept in a hollow tooth.

A quick and dirty way of concealing something in your mouth without worry about any possible bulge is to keep it in a wad of chewing gum. Chew on it gently, so as not to destroy your material, and you'll probably pass inspection.

CLOTHING

Seams are natural hiding places for small objects. Only a thorough search will uncover material hidden this way. A standard security police technique is to search clothing by crumpling the seams while shaking out the article.

Shoulder pads are also fairly good hides. You need little sewing ability to cut one open along a seam, insert your material, and repair the seam.

Whenever you have to sew up a garment, it's important not only to match the thread, but the mode of stitching. This varies a lot between countries, and failing to match the stitch can betray you. So can removing the seam entirely and replacing it with a stitching style not appropriate to the label.

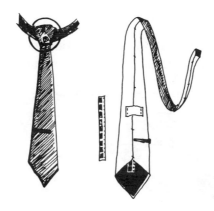

A small item can be in the knot of the tie. Because a necktie is a flattened tube, it's usually open at both ends. A strip of film will fit.

The belt will hide some flat objects. Undo the stitching, insert your material, and sew it up again, using a matching thread.

Carrying something inside your shorts is also practical, if you don't expect a strip search. Sewing it into the waistband of your shorts or trousers is another way, if the object is flat and thin.

Carrying inside the rectum is a short term proposition, because sooner or later it must come out.

A wallet is a natural, and many of them are made of several layers of leather or nylon. Inserting something between these layers will hide it from a superficial search.

Trouser cuffs are mostly out of style, and the opportunity to hide something in them scarcely exists anymore.

Hollow heels are workable, but not in the way you see in the movies. Don't even try to take the heel off, because reattaching it solidly enough to permit walking and running will be a problem unless you want the job to be permanent. Instead, pry up the liner of your shoe or boot. When you get to the heel, use an X-Acto knife to make a cavity.[1]

You can also hide very flat objects between the upper and lower soles of your boots.[2] Don't glue the two soles together, though, unless they were originally joined with glue. Use matching thread. This requires a stout needle.

ACCESSORIES

Using other personal items may or may not be prudent. A ballpoint or felt tip pen will hide small items such as .22 cartridges, and it's even possible to leave the point in as a disguise. The pen will continue to work for a short time.[3]

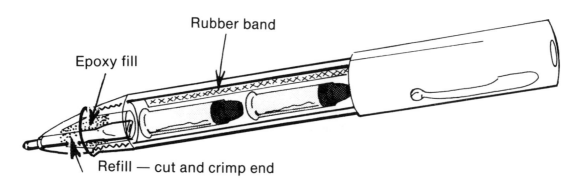

Using a hollowed out pack of cigarettes may be a good idea, if you don't smoke and nobody tries to bum one from you. Hollowing out cigarettes risks burning up your material and possibly creating a hazard.

One or more full-length cigarettes improves your chances!

A loaf of bread makes a halfway good hide. It's cheap enough to be expendable, so buy two. One is for practice and the other's for real. A loaf of pre-sliced bread is best, because you risk the least in taking it apart and hollowing out the centers of the slices without leaving traces of your work. The only problem that might come is if you have to go through an electronic gate and have a weapon inside.[4]

If you're skilled with tools, you may want to try concealing your material inside the platen of a typewriter.[5] Much depends on the make of typewriter you have. Some brands are easier than others to disassemble.

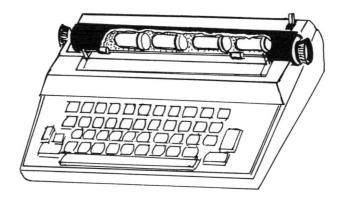

We'll cover vehicles in the next chapter, but one accessory is worth a look at here: the bicycle pump.[6] Many of these have removable endcaps, and the interior compartment can serve as a hide. You may not be able to use a full stroke, though, if you have to demonstrate that it works, and if you have the entire inside filled to prevent rattles, you may not be able to pump air at all.

NOTES

1. *Duty Free,* Michael Connor, (Boulder, Colorado, Paladin Press, 1983) p. 41.

2. *Ibid.,* p. 33.

3. *Sneak It Through,* Michael Connor, (Boulder, Colorado, Paladin Press, 1984) p. 12.

4. *Ibid.,* pp. 15-16.

5. *Ibid.,* pp. 8-9.

6. *Ibid.,* p. 8.

USING VEHICLES

Using a vehicle is often more rewarding than trying to hide material on the person, because of the greater space available and because it's much more time consuming to search a vehicle. Smugglers and spies use vehicles regularly.

During the 1920's, the U.S. Military Intelligence Service devised a plan to build an espionage organization in Japan. One of the features of this plan was a clandestine transmitter concealed in the gas tank of a car. This feature did not see the light of day, because subsequent events made it obsolete.

Greville Wynn, the British businessman who let himself be used by his country's espionage agency, MI-6, was equipped with a large house trailer that contained a secret compartment. The plan was for him to smuggle Colonel Oleg Penkovsky, a Soviet officer and defector-in-place, out from behind the Iron Curtain. He and Penkovsky were arrested before they could work the plan.

The "French Connection" heroin case in New York concerned a large stash of heroin concealed in the rocker panels of the smuggler's car. This frustrated the police until they seized the car and dismantled it thoroughly to reveal the hiding place.

These are three instances that became public knowledge, one because a former intelligence officer revealed it in his memoirs, and two because of police action and public trials. There are doubtless many thousands of other instances which remain unknown.

Modern vehicles provide many opportunities to hide material. Some are easier than others, and some require very specialized tools and abilities. As with other types of hides, these will give good protection from a quick or casual search, but are of little use in the event of a thorough professional dismantling. Let's look over motor vehicles with an eye towards concealment.

CHASSIS

Generally, the chassis consists of box or H-shaped members. A few cars, such as the Citroen 2CV, have some tubular accessories fitted to the chassis. A box with a magnet provides the simplest and most convenient method of attaching something to a car's chassis. This is the same sort of box people use to keep a spare key concealed behind the bumper. It's also one of the least secure, because a quick inspection with a mirror can reveal it. To help avoid this, a layer of crud on the underside of the car helps.

To simulate crud, use a can of spray undercoat, available in any auto supply shop or K-Mart, and coat the box. Drive the vehicle over a dusty road to pick up road dirt quickly.

Concealing inside a frame member requires some cutting and welding. A good accessory to have at this point is gun blue, which you use to dull the bright shine of the weld and any scratches on the rest of the work area. You can pick this up at a gun shop or a K-Mart. Apply it with a cotton swab. It works almost instantly. A coat of oil, grease, or undercoating finishes the disguise.

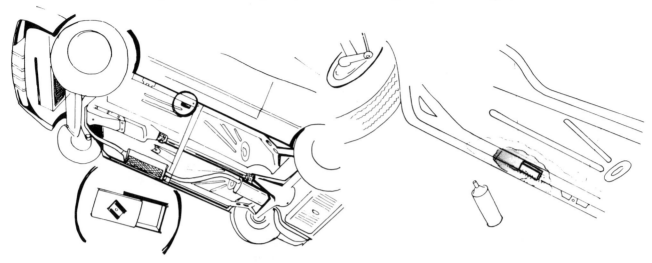

Attaching material to the top of the muffler is one rude and crude technique.[1] Some wire or heavy-duty aluminum tape will work, but the material must be covered up with road crud, real or simulated. The problem with this method comes when you try to use undercoating or any petroleum product. The muffler becomes hot, and you'll be trailing a streamer of smoke down the road. Don't even try to attach anything to the catalytic converter. That becomes even hotter.

Using the gas tank is a better idea. You can either wedge something on top of it, or build a secret compartment inside. A lot depends on the amount of bulk you have to conceal.

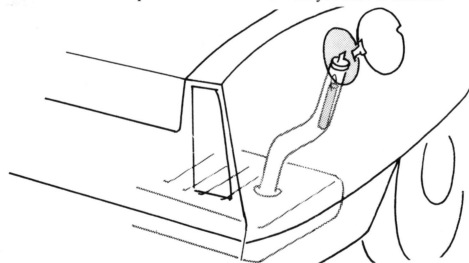

One quick way to use the gas tank is to construct a small tubular compartment that will drop down your filler tube until the first kink.[2]

If your trip is short enough so that you won't need to gas up before arriving, you can use this method successfully. Of course, whatever you're hiding must not be vulnerable to gas fumes.

You could take your gas tank off, cut it apart, and build a false compartment in it, but that's the hard way. Your best bet if you need a lot of space is to empty out your gas tank and use it all for the secret compartment. Install another, smaller tank under a seat and run your gas line from that.

Using the hubcaps to conceal anything is such an old idea that it's stale. So is the technique of putting contraband inside the tires. These are probably the first two places anyone would check.

FALSE LINES AND STRUCTURES

There are so many makes of cars, all with their emission control devices, that almost nobody can remember the layouts of all of them. This provides you the opportunity to "install" a number of totally fake lines, hoses, wires, canisters, and other material both under the hood and under the body. Probably the main problem will be finding room.

There are just two rules to remember. Each item or line must go somewhere, come from somewhere, or seem to be attached to something. The other is that it must look "automotive." Auto parts have a certain style, which varies somewhat from one make to another. Extra items you put under the hood must match the others in finish and color, for example. They must fit in. An exception is if your vehicle is old, and has had many spare parts fitted that were not O.E.M. However, an older car has fewer emission control devices.

There are several ways to make fake parts fit in. One is to have it wired to something. A blank terminal on the fuse box will do. If you make sure that the wire running from your fake part is well insulated and doesn't ground out the circuit, you can even have the wire connected to a live terminal.

Another way is to have hoses connecting it to something. You can use one of the existing hose circuits for this. Cut a hose at a convenient point, and install a tee connector.

The tee connects to the hose running to your spurious component. Make sure your hose is blocked off at one end, as you don't want to be introducing a leak into the functioning circuit.

Between emission control devices and after market add-ons, there are many ways to construct secret hiding places under the hood and body of the vehicle. To help this, add on a few legitimate extras yourself, to give the under hood space a more cluttered look.

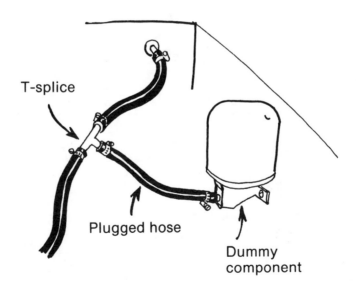

T-splice

Plugged hose

Dummy component

During a search, don't even try to explain the function of any component if asked. Simply shrug, shake your head, and mutter, "Must be emission control or somp'n."

Yet another way to hide material is to hollow out real items under the hood. There is a way to put contraband into a battery, but this is difficult. A better way is to take off the emission control devices and empty them out. Fill them with your contraband and replace them, making sure you cover them with a film of oil and dust to cover your work. Your engine will run well without the emission control devices. In fact, it'll run better. Police and customs agents inspect for contraband, not faulty emissions, and your system's being inoperative will pass unnoticed.

INSIDE THE CAR

The ash tray is a good place for a quick and small hide.[3] A piece of metal makes a false bottom, under which your contraband fits. One point to watch is that the material must withstand heat. The other is that the false bottom must be very obviously used. If you don't smoke, "borrow" some cigarette butts and ashes from a friend, or raid somebody's garbage can. In an emergency, walk into a diner with a plastic bag and empty some ash trays into it.

The visor serves as a hiding place for small objects.[4] If you undo the seam, remove enough stuffing to allow your material to slip in without causing a bulge, and resew, you'll have a small but fairly secure hide.

The tubes behind the dash can hold a lot, and they're not obviously accessible. Using the heater or air conditioner hoses and ducts for small items is fairly secure.[5] It helps a lot if you're driving in mild weather and don't need to turn either system on.

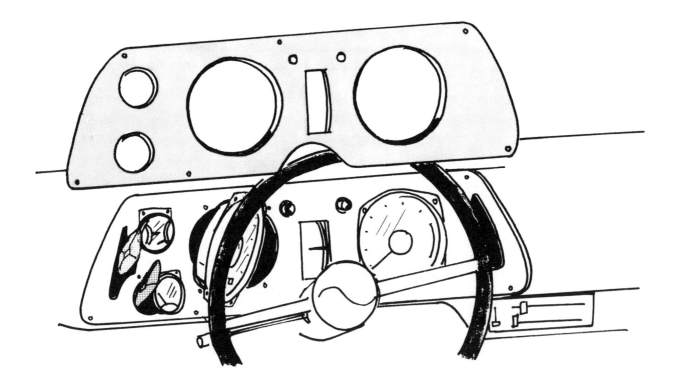

The dash is usually a good place to explore for hides.[6] Most of it is hollow, and removing one or two gauges will reveal spaces behind them. You can squeeze a number of small items in between the wires.

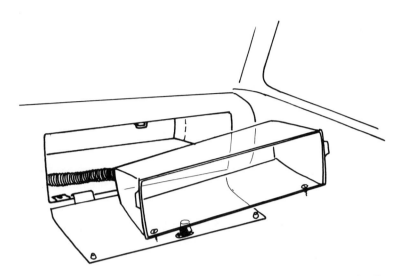

Remove the glove compartment liner to see what's behind it. In some cars the liner comes out easily from the front. Usually, there's not as much wiring and tubing behind that part of the dash, because the instruments and radio are on the other side. This gives you a good opportunity to stash "stuff" behind the liner.

The gear lever and knob are worth a look, because removing the knob and drilling out the lever creates a narrow tubular hide for small items such as .22 ammo.[7]

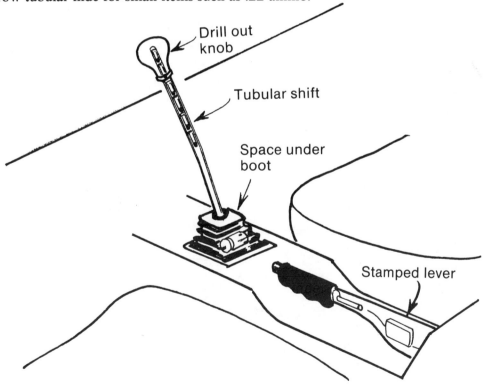

Drill out knob

Tubular shift

Space under boot

Stamped lever

If you have "four on the floor" your lever has a boot between it and the transmission hump. This boot is easily removable to permit insertion of material.

Emergency brake levers are usually pressed steel, and hollow. This allows some space for small objects.

Armrests are bulky, with enough space to construct a hidden compartment.[8] You may have to remove the door panels to get at the screws holding them on, though. This can give you double security.

If what you need to hide will fit inside a hollowed out armrest, you can place it there, knowing that a searcher will remove your door panel, find nothing hidden behind it, and possibly stop his search before unscrewing your armrest.

The car seats are upholstered, and sometimes the upholstery is exposed, as underneath car seats. In other instances, there may be a panel covering the foam in the seat back. If this panel unscrews easily, hiding material behind it will not be a major operation. If you want a little extra security, a set of seat covers will make the easy access less obvious.

You can conceal a lot under a car's carpet, even if the car's a cheapie with only thin rubber mats. An additional way is to get a set of floor mats. The thicker, plusher ones offer a lot of space to conceal material between layers.

For truly small objects, taking the rubber pads off the brake, accelerator, and clutch pedals will reveal stowage for small and flat objects. These are usually difficult enough to remove and put on that a searcher's unlikely to look under them.

BODYWORK

Fender wells offer good hiding places, but not if the object's just screwed on or attached magnetically. If you're skilled at auto body work, you can install an additional panel in the rear fender wells, which need less room for wheel movement. This is a semi-permanent installation, and the material has to be valuable enough to justify the work you put in.

Between the fender wells and the passenger compartments are internal wells, narrow channels that run inside the trunk or under the hood. In some instances, these are narrow and dark enough that it's possible simply to drop small objects in to hide them. It's possible to disguise the access by constructing small panels to cover them, and painting the panels to appear as part of the bodywork. A final, "touch-up" layer of dirt will finish the job.

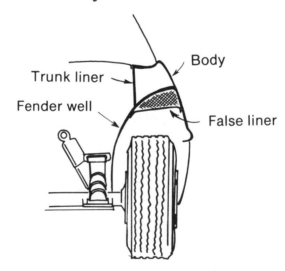

If the car's got a vinyl roof, the "beaten roof" technique will work. First, remove the vinyl. Usually, the glue will dissolve with the manufacturer's recommended solvent. Then, pound down several shallow compartments in the roof metal. Be sure that these hides don't reach down far enough to deform the headliner inside the car. Line the vinyl with a thin layer of glass fiber cloth and epoxy to maintain its shape in the roof line, and reattach it to the roof of the car.[9] This gives a semi-permanent hide that, although troublesome to arrange, is fairly secure.

Removing the headliner will offer a more convenient access to the area under the roof. If you can do this neatly, you can hide things with no loss of security. If a searcher goes as far as removing the headliner, he'd discover any indentations in your roof, anyway. You can use a thin sheet of metal to produce a hard, flat surface to any searcher who pokes your headliner.

THE READY WEAPON

If you need to hide a weapon in your car, yet need easy and quick access, you're going to have to compromise. A secure hiding place is hard to reach. A quick one offers little security and may be very easy to find. One compromise is the console between the seats. These consoles usually have compartments with lids, very much like glove boxes. A handgun will usually fit very easily in one, leaving space for a speedloader or a couple of extra clips.

One way to add a little extra security is to disguise the lid. Build a tray on top if it, so that you can store your spare change and cigarettes yet flip it up to reach your handgun.

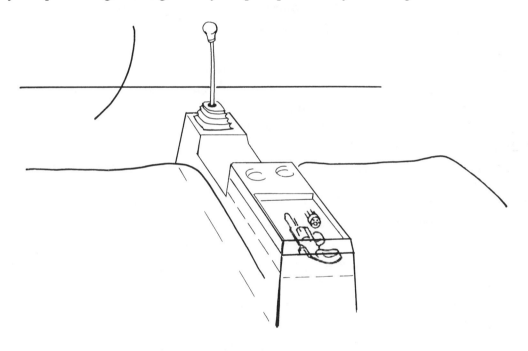

NOTES

1. *Duty Free,* Michael Connor, (Boulder, Colorado, Paladin Press, 1983) p. 10.

2. *Ibid.,* p. 11.

3. *Ibid.,* p. 4.

4. *Ibid.,* p. 10.

5. *Ibid.,* p. 9.

6. *Sneak It Through,* Michael Connor, (Boulder, Colorado, Paladin Press, 1984) p. 62.

7. *Ibid.,* p. 61.

8. *Duty Free,* p. 5.

9. *Ibid.,* pp. 21-23.

A QUICK LOOK AT SMUGGLING

The philosophy and risks of smuggling are worth a good look, because many who start careers in smuggling don't consider the consequences. The first question for you to answer is: "Who are you?"

Some people have special advantages in smuggling. Those who frequently make overseas trips, for example, have their travel arrangements ready made. Airline employees, for example, have a conduit for the illicit importation of contraband. The recent Eastern Airlines case gives us a good example.[1] A Columbian drug smuggling ring had been operating for several years, with an enlistment of Eastern Airlines employees.

Such a development isn't surprising. Commercial aircraft have many hiding places for kilos of drugs. Airline employees regularly pass through customs, and it's understandable if customs agents aren't as diligent in checking them out as they are with passengers. The interface of activity on the airfield allows passing of contraband completely out of the sight of customs agents. This requires the collaboration of ground crew, but this is easy to obtain, as the Eastern Airlines case showed.

If you look reasonably "straight," that is, respectable, your chances of passing customs inspection are far better than if you are fuzzy and scuzzy. Law officers are as narrow-minded as anyone else, and as subject to stereotyping. They'll jump all over a "hippie" type, but the neat looking man in a three-piece suit will usually pass unmolested. If he comes under suspicion, the investigation will begin with polite questions, not the snarling interrogation that a less "respectable" person would face.

Thus, we see that certain statuses give us forms of immunity, and we don't have to obey the laws with the same diligence as do the rest of the people.

Police officers also enjoy a certain immunity. Police who live and patrol near borders have special advantages. They and their families can cross the border themselves.

Customs agents have special advantages that even the police don't enjoy. This is why we hardly ever see an instance of a customs agent arrested for smuggling. They never get caught. In fact, they're very well insulated from discovery. A customs agent will not do the smuggling himself. He'll simply collaborate with a smuggler, and look the other way when the smuggler crosses the border.

Diplomats have very special status. Because of the Vienna Accords, anyone with a diplomatic passport is immune from search, seizure, and arrest. A diplomatic passport is practically a "license to kill." Diplomats regularly smuggle in contraband, either for themselves or for their countries. There's no problem because customs agents are forbidden to open their luggage or even to ask them if they have anything to declare. Espionage equipment regularly comes in through the "diplomatic bag." This is not necessarily a bag, but is often a huge packing crate. It can contain anything, literally anything, including weapons, drugs, and even a body. Over twenty years ago, Egyptian diplomats tried to smuggle an anesthetized espionage agent out of Italy in a diplomat's trunk. Because the agent wasn't heavily drugged, he revived and made enough noise at Fiumicino airport to attract the attention of an Italian customs officer, who stopped the effort.

Civilians who live near borders have special status, although it's entirely unofficial. They know the geography very well, and some of them have been in the contraband business for generations. In Europe's Pyrenee mountains, for example, the local people have been smuggling for centuries, regularly violating the border between France and Spain.

EXPLOITATION

There are two ways of exploiting other people for smuggling, wittingly and unwittingly. It's possible to ask someone else to carry a package across a border for you. This can be risky or dangerous. In some situations, there is strict currency control, and a limit on the amount of currency one person can carry out of the country. Dividing a large amount between two people can "keep it legal."

Certain contraband items, such as cocaine, are never legal, and asking someone to carry it across exposes them to risk. You would not ask a friend to do so. This brings us to the unwitting accomplice.

Placing contraband in someone else's luggage is one way to do it. One technique for this is to change name tags on pieces of luggage that look alike. Another is dropping it surreptitiously into a woman's handbag. Retrieving it later requires only a staged "accident," in which someone bumps into her and spills the handbag contents onto the floor.

A commonly used technique is to fix contraband onto a motor vehicle making regular trips across a frontier. It may be the car of a traveling salesman, or a delivery van. The main requirement is that the border guards not check the vehicle carefully each crossing. A magnetic box holding the goods will stick behind the bumper or to the chassis, for removal across the border. If the driver stops for coffee, it gives the smuggler an opportunity to plant the contraband. Following him across the border will give the smuggler another chance at the vehicle the next time the driver stops.

Smugglers have to beware of cultural clashes, unwitting actions that might draw unwanted attention. For example, in Spain and Soviet Russia, publications such as *Playboy* and *Hustler* are viewed as hardcore pornography. Unless this policy has loosened up by the time this book appears in print, any copies you take with you will be confiscated. You'll get a special look from customs guards, who might search your luggage to determine if you're bringing in other sexual contraband.

In some locales, cameras mark you for suspicion. Be careful if you go near any military installations. The camera hanging innocently around your neck may be "prima facie" evidence against you!

PSYCHOLOGY

Smuggling can be emotionally trying. You can wind up with labored breathing and heart palpitations at the moment of truth, when you have to look a customs agent in the eye and state that you have "nothing to declare." One expert in the field advises doing some "dummy runs" to overcome your anxiety.[2] The reason for this is very clear. If you can train yourself to face a stressful situation repeatedly, without heavy consequences coming down on you, you'll extinguish the anxiety you feel. By passing through customs and dealing with the border guards while you have nothing to fear, you can build up a confidence that you'd lack if you were worried that a zealous agent might find contraband hidden in your luggage.

One problem with dummy runs is expense. If the dummy run merely takes you across the border a few miles from where you live, as in Northern Ireland, it's not a problem. If you have to cross the ocean, it can be costly.

Mental rehearsal is another technique, and it costs nothing. Running through a customs inspection in your mind repeatedly will help you to plan how to meet it, and how to answer questions. This will also help in deconditioning yourself from the grip of anxiety.

Using psychology against customs agents will help somewhat, if they're not absolutely suspicious. If you're smuggling in material which you can carry in your luggage, try to carry it in a container which doesn't seem to come apart. A seemingly solid subject that must be damaged to examine it thoroughly will serve as a deterrent, compared to anything which can be easily opened. Hiding dope in the battery compartment of a radio is not very smart. Concealing it in a cast statue is.

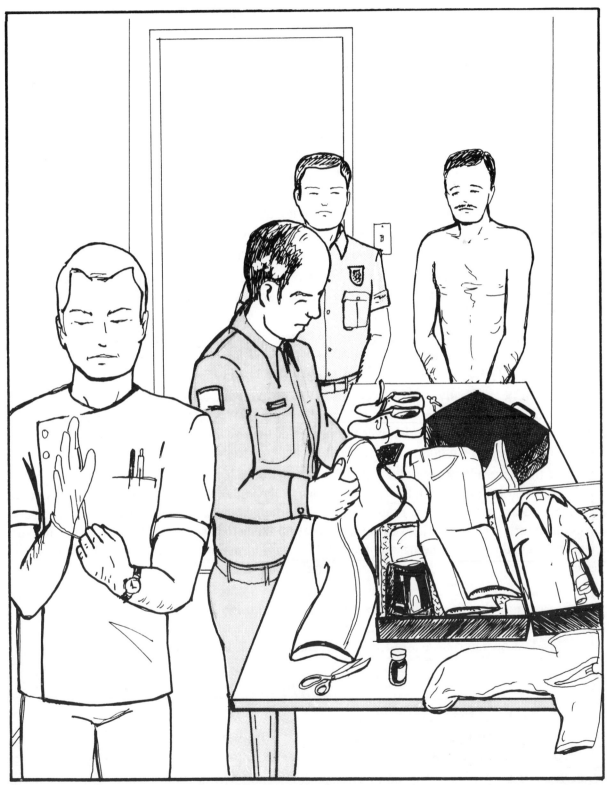

This will work only so far. If the customs authorities have reason to suspect you, such as having been "tipped off," they'll take you into a back room and show you how thorough a search can be. Customs officials usually are the only police agents allowed to search without a warrant.

The search can involve thorough dismantling of your luggage and everything in it. Slitting the lining of each suitcase is not too extreme a measure in the effort to find contraband. Neither is breaking apart every container you are carrying. Contraband might be in a shaving cream can or camera.

You may be asked to submit to a strip search, in which you literally strip to the skin while customs agents go over your clothing seam by seam, inch by inch. The search can involve close examination of your body, such as combing through your hair, looking into your ears and mouth, and even rubber gloved inspection of your rectum.

TREACHERY

One obvious point to observe when traveling is never to accept anything from anyone who asks you to carry a small package for him. This theme has been featured in so many films that even a child should understand why. The several possibilities are not always obvious. Let's review them quickly:

• A smuggler tries to delegate the risk to you. You carry the contraband, while he accompanies you on the trip or takes a later flight. If you're caught, you're holding the bag.

• An espionage agent has some material he needs smuggled, and can't do it himself because he's known to the authorities. You, as an innocent traveler, are a perfect carrier. If you don't believe this, watch some old Alfred Hitchcock films.

• The person asking for your help may be an "agent-provocateur," drumming up business for the cops. A customs agent with an arrest record that's "down" for the month may be trying to beef up his statistics. An easy way for him to do this is to use a sleazeball to "set up" otherwise innocent people.

You have to be especially watchful regarding the people with whom you deal if you're a serious smuggler. This is because there is truly no "honor among thieves." Many of them are treacherous to the core, and would willingly crawl over the bodies of their dying mothers to rape their sisters. The only factor that keeps them honest in their dealings with confederates is the fear of reprisal.

Some of these sleazebags are in the contraband business by leave of the police. They deal in illegal arms, drugs, or stolen goods with the full knowledge of the authorities in their country. This is because they have a "deal" with the authorities, a reciprocal arrangement in which they're allowed to stay in business in return for tipping them off to a proportion of their business contacts. In other instances, they have criminal charges pending, and the police exact information from them in lieu of prosecution. This leaves you very vulnerable, unless you're impeccably "connected."

The dealer/informer will alert the cops or the customs agents to a certain number of independent operators each month. His truly profitable dealings are with the "mob," and he dares not inform on them. He knows that if he did, he'd be floating in the river, or buried in the desert, shortly afterward. The independent operator, once arrested, cannot take reprisals, and this makes him a good target.

MONEY

One aspect often overlooked by would-be smugglers is the need to pay for the contraband. Bringing in the goods is the second problem. Taking out the money to pay for it is the necessary prerequisite.

Americans usually don't suffer customs inspection when leaving the country. They can have a suitcase full of bills and not worry about molestation on this side of the border. On the other side, customs may or may not be rigorous. It all depends upon the country. British and French customs usually let through Americans who state that they have nothing to declare without further delay. In

Britain, however, an Irish surname or accent may cause extra attention, whatever the nationality of the passport.

Only independent operators have to worry about taking money through customs in a suitcase. The heavy-duty rings have other methods, such as dummy corporations sending electroninc fund transfers through legitimate banks.

Payment can also be in precious stones. This is a particularly attractive method of smuggling value across a border because precious stones take so little space, and a million dollar's worth of diamonds will fit in a toothpaste tube.

SMUGGLING FOR FUN AND PROFIT

Smuggling in an extra bottle of duty-free booze is one thing; bringing in a heavy amount of drugs is another. The main hazard, as we've seen, is not casual customs inspection. Although they have the authority to do so, customs agents simply can't strip search everyone who passes through their lines. They'd tie up traffic for days. Instead, they rely upon spot checks, deterrence, and a network of informers.

If you're thinking of smuggling anything, consider the risks realistically. There's little risk in small items. Personally owned jewelry or an undeclared camera are in the same class as the extra bottle of alcohol. You probably won't be caught, but even if you are, the customs agent will almost surely accept your plea of forgetfulness. The customs agents are interested in collecting fees, not spending the government's money imprisoning people for petty offenses.

If you're into heavy-duty smuggling, the main danger is from informers, not casual inspection. Your method of concealment will be such that you defeat or deter superficial efforts, but if an informer blows the whistle on you, you won't be able to avoid detection and arrest. Anticipate your risks and act accordingly.

NOTES

1. Associated Press, February 12, 1986.
2. *Duty Free,* Michael Connor, (Boulder, Colorado, Paladin Press, 1983) pp. 57-58.

UNCONVENTIONAL MEANS

Permanent and personal hiding places have their uses, but sometimes they'll be inaccessible or impractical. You may expect to be searched, or you may have searchers going over your home with a fine-tooth comb. We've already seen that truly determined and skilled searchers can find practically anything if it's there to be found.

You then need to "ditch" your material so that nobody'll find it. There are several ways of doing so, and each is worth a close look to assess its advantages and disadvantages. They're all stashes away from home, and sometimes very far away. Note that most of the methods outlined limit you to relatively small and light parcels.

COIN LOCKERS

These are available in every bus, train, and airline terminal. Some are in subway stations. You insert a coin, drop off your material, and walk away with the key.

The advantages are low cost and instant access. You walk in, drop off your stuff, and walk out. You need make no prior preparation.

However, the locker may be rented to you for a limited period only. Be sure to inquire before stashing any material this way. In some instances, there will be a sign on the locker giving this information.

If the locker is at an airport, be extremely discreet about stashing drugs, weapons or explosives. If the locker is on the concourse, and you have to pass through a security checkpoint to reach it, forget it. If it's not, there's still a risk. Many airport police use explosives detection dogs, and if it's an international airport, customs officials will have their dogs check for drugs. A dog being walked through the corridor by his handler may "alert" to the material in your locker. Indeed, at some airports there are regular sniff searches of banks of lockers to detect contraband.

Airport and bus depot lockers are also small. They're suitable for storing a suitcase or two, but that's it.

MAIL IT TO YOURSELF

One way to get rid of some material awhile is to mail it to yourself. It'll get lost in the channels of the postal service for several days to several weeks, depending on the class of service. Parcel Post takes the longest, but even First Class can take a week. The maximum amount you can send by post office is 70 pounds, and the cost can be as much as $26, if mailed from one coast to another.

This puts your material in the custody of the U.S. Government, one of the safest, if least efficient, ways to go. It's also not extremely expensive.

But there can be disadvantages, depending on how you handle the problem. First, it's obvious that anything you mail to yourself at your home address comes back to you. If your home is being watched, this method isn't secure at all.

You can mail it to a friend. This can be a problem. You will have to arrange it in advance with a friend you can trust, and in the riskier situations, you can't trust many people. One obvious fact is that the friend will want to know what's in the package or envelope. What do you tell him? You'll probably decide to use a service that's professionally incurious.

GENERAL DELIVERY

Another way is to address the parcel to yourself in care of "General Delivery." Every town has a General Delivery service, and in its simplest form they hold it for you at the main post office when you address it to: John Blank, c/o General Delivery, Anytown, USA 10000.

One problem is that you must show I.D. to claim it. This can be a problem if you've sent it to yourself under an assumed name. If you're on somebody's "wanted" list, you may find it awkward to use your real name. Another problem with General Delivery is that the post office will hold it only ten days. After that, it's either "Return To Sender" or the Dead Letter Office.

THE POST OFFICE BOX

Yet another way is to rent a post office box. The rate for the smallest is $11 per six months. It's only necessary to rent the smallest size for this purpose, because any packages that won't fit will result in a notice in your box that a package is waiting for you at the pick-up window. Of course, if you repeatedly get large envelopes and packages, you may be asked to rent a larger box.

The big advantage of a P.O. box is that you can leave material in there for as long as your rental exists. You're not pressured to pick it up in a limited period.

One possibly big disadvantage of renting a post office box is that it's illegal to rent under an assumed name, and the clerk will ask you for I.D. when you sign the rental agreement. This can be inconvenient if you require anonymity.

MAIL DROPS

There's a class of "service industry" that's purposely and professionally incurious about its clients. These are the mail drops.

A mail drop, also known as an "accommodation address," "secret address," etc., is a place where you can receive mail under whatever name you wish. People rent mail drops so that they can:

(1) Receive mail they wish to keep secret from members of their households.

(2) Receive mail without the sender knowing their home address.

These can involve all sorts of purposes. Not all are illegal. Some renters use their secret addresses for correspondence of a torrid sexual nature. Others engage in various frauds and rip-offs. Yet others are commercial clients, using a "blind address" when advertising for hired help.

Operators of mail drops don't want to know anything their clients don't choose to tell them, because they know that some of the purposes are illegal. It boils down to "don't look too close." Knowing would make them accessories, and consequently, they're discreet. As long as you pay the fee, they'll provide the service. They usually don't insist on I.D.

A private address of this sort is much more expensive than a post office box. The charges run about ten dollars per month for the basic service. Extra services, such as forwarding mail to another address, can cost extra for the service or a nominal charge for the envelopes and the postage required.

Some mail drops operate from post office boxes themselves. This provides an aura of anonymity which some dislike. Others provide a street address, which doesn't advertise the "blind" aspect. Another advantage of a mail drop with a street address is that you can use it to receive packages delivered by United Parcel Service or other commercial carriers. These have trouble delivering to post office boxes.

The main point about a mail drop is that the operator will do what you want done, as long as you pay the fee. This means that he'll hold your mail for as long as you wish, or forward it to another address after a certain time if that's what you instruct him to do. Generally, mail drop operators don't like to hold on to mail for a long time, and some ask their customers to pick up at least once a week. However, if your rental's paid up and the volume of mail they have to store for you isn't excessive, they'll generally tolerate it.

Make your arrangement in advance if you're going to expect long term storage. The "out of the country" story is a safe one. Tell the operator that you're out of the country most of the time, and that's why you don't have an address here. You're willing to pay for many months in advance, but you won't be able to pick up regularly. If you look reasonably clean cut, you should have no problems. This is an utterly safe and discreet way of getting a package of papers or other material "lost" awhile.

The only possible compromises to your security are if someone follows you when you make the initial rental of the mail drop service, or when you pick up your mail. Another can be if you pay by check. Cash or money order will safeguard your anonymity.

A directory of mail drops is available from:

LOOMPANICS UNLIMITED

PO BOX 1197

PORT TOWNSEND, WA 98368

MINI-STORAGE

If you must store bulky or heavy material, use a mini-storage. A mini-warehouse will rent you a storage room for a monthly rate that will vary with the area of the country and the size of the room. The smallest ones are about four feet square, and rent for about eight dollars per month. Much larger and more expensive rooms are available, and if you have a huge amount to store you can rent several.

Because these facilities are privately owned, their operators follow the same practices as with mail drops. They don't really want to know your business, and are mainly concerned with collecting the rent. They don't necessarily want to see your I.D., but many will ask you to sign a contract, which can include a "cleaning deposit."

USE YOUR IMAGINATION

With so many off premises hiding places available, you should not have much trouble getting good security for the material you want to hide. In even a medium size city, there are so many possibilities available that you can make some excellent choices. With your hiding place away from home, you'll easily frustrate any searchers, and the only way they'll find your hide is to torture it out of you.

You also need to protect yourself against discovery. Police agencies raid storage facilities on search warrants. They find out about them because the renter has the address written down, or he keeps rental receipts in his home. It does no good to rent a mail drop or mini-storage under an alias, then save the receipts where they're easily found. Any paperwork trail will compromise security, and simply give it away to anyone who sees the paper.

CONCEALED WEAPONS

Concealing weapons on the person is becoming more widely spread today. For obvious reasons, this practice brings little publicity in proportion to the number of people who "carry." Only when there's violence does it make the headlines, as in the Bernhard Goetz case.

There are several legitimate reasons for "carrying," and they all center around self-protection:

(1) Police officers, of course, carry weapons, and plainclothes officers carry them concealed.

(2) Civilians who carry large amounts of money, or who carry valuables, as in the case of jewelers, often feel the need to be armed.

(3) Civilians who live in high risk areas often feel that they need more protection than simply using their fists. "The cops are never there when you need them" is the realistic justification for carrying a concealed weapon.

The plight of the armed citizen becomes severe in a locale which has both a high risk of mugging and a gun law forbidding concealed weapons. Some gun laws are so restrictive that they outlaw weapons altogether. This places the citizen concerned about self-protection right in a "Catch-22." If he obeys the law, he's left defenseless against armed thugs. If he disobeys, he risks prosecution. Many resolve this problem in a practical manner: "I'd rather be tried by twelve than carried by six." The wisdom of this statement needs no further comment.

THE PURPOSE

Carrying a weapon concealed provides one great tactical advantage. The assailant does not know that his intended victim is armed, and consequently the victim can take advantage of surprise. If the assault is a robbery, the victim can draw his weapon when told to hand over his wallet. In other cases, the victim can choose the opportunity.

An additional purpose for concealment comes when the law itself outlaws either guns or their concealed carry. An irony of Twentieth Century American life is that the law often makes the potential victim as much of a "criminal" as his assailant. To carry a weapon concealed helps to avoid hassles with the law, but if ever there's a need to use it, the urgency is such that legal questions become almost irrelevant.

THE LAW

American laws vary from state to state, and from one jurisdiction to another within each state. Their enforcement is capricious. Ironically, the jurisdictions with the fewest restrictive gun laws are the ones with the lowest crime rates. In a "combat zone," such as New York City, mere possession of a firearm of any sort without a police permit is illegal, and even air rifles are outlawed.

An additional hazard to the person who defends himself with a concealed weapon is the compounding of a felony. Some states, such as New York and California, have laws that classify any death that occurs while committing a felony as "Murder One." The purpose of this law is to make felons such as armed robbers fully accountable for their actions, and prevent any "copping out," such as claiming that a traffic death while escaping was accidental. This technicality of the law can have a pernicious effect on the armed citizen in some instances.

In locales where mere possession of a weapon without a permit is a felony, a citizen who kills his assailant is automatically liable to a charge of "Murder One," and in fact a few people have been arrested for exactly that in New York City. This is the point that any citizen who plans to "carry" in such locales should keep in mind. The effect of such a law is that any defender who stays in the area to answer the questions of the police is in deep trouble. This is why police find cadavers killed without apparent motives and without witnesses. These corpses are the residue of aborted stickups.

Now that we've covered the theory, let's get into the meat of the subject.

THE CHOICE OF WEAPONS

The choice is between firearms and edged weapons. We won't get into chemical weapons or electronic "stun guns" for one excellent reason: they're not always reliable. Police experience with tear gas sprays shows that they work only about 70% of the time. "Stun guns" cause pain and shock, but do not paralyze, and some people seem to be immune to their effects. Ironically, some cities and states have rushed to ban stun guns even before their effectiveness or lack thereof has been clearly established.

KNIVES

Knives are simple, light, inexpensive, and easily available. They need no other components, such as ammunition, and except for switchblades and other retractable or folding knives, have no moving parts to get out of order.

Knives are contact weapons. It's necessary to be very close for effectiveness. This means that usually a knife is not an even match for a gun. If you're armed with a knife, and your attacker has a firearm, you're outclassed. In very close quarters, however, you may have an even chance.

Knife throwing isn't a worthwhile technique. It takes too long to master. You can use the knife against only one assailant and once it leaves your hand you've lost your weapon.

You can use a knife for a slashing or a stabbing attack. Both can be lethal, if they strike vital organs or cut major blood vessels. A slashing attack at the throat can be lethal, cutting the jugular veins and the carotid arteries. A stabbing attack under the breastbone threatens the heart and major blood vessels, especially if the user swings the blade from one side to the other after insertion. The problem is that response to a knife wound is often slow. People shot often don't drop instantly, and those slashed or stabbed take even longer to go down.

Physical response can be slow, but psychological response may be very rapid. A mugger, seeing his own blood gushing onto the concrete, may suddenly lose all heart for the encounter. The sight of blood has nothing to do with the lethality of the injury. The problem is that this is hard to predict. Some people are psychologically tough, while others fold up immediately at the sight of blood.

Although you can use any sort of edged weapon for lethal effect, the best type for concealed carry is the fighting dagger, often known as the "commando knife."

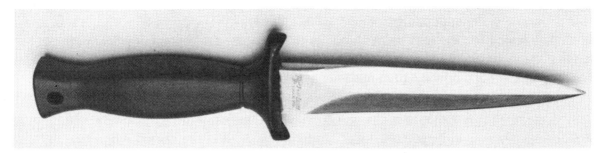

This is a well balanced, light knife about nine inches long, with a double-edged blade. It lends itself well to either a stabbing attack or to slashing forehand or backhand. A single-edged knife will do for slashing attacks, but you have to twist your wrist to change directions.

A type of knife that's especially suited for concealment is the plastic or glass fiber knife. These are made by Choate Machine & Tool Co., PO Box 218, Bald Knob, AR, and sold for less than ten dollars. They weigh from under an ounce to almost two ounces, and are between seven and eight inches long. All have lanyard holes in the end of the grip. This allows a carrying lanyard or a wrist loop.

Some are known as "Executive Letter Openers." Another type is the "Ace of Spades," a short and stubby double-edged weapon that fits in the palm of the hand. The "Executive Ice Scraper" is a device with a straight blade, which is actually useful for scraping ice from a car windshield. Striking someone, with it held in the fist, will produce a nasty gash.

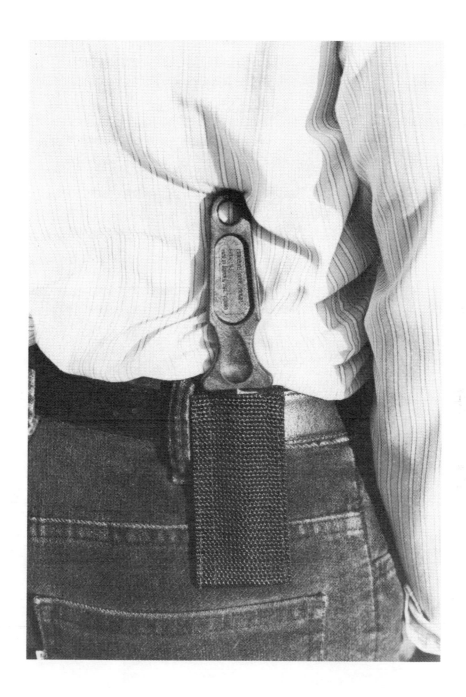

Carry can be in several ways. A belt scabbard is available for the "letter openers." Other ways are down the neck on a string, under the watch band, taped to the thigh, ankle, or under the armpit, and tucked into the boot or sock. Other ways of carrying are in a pocket, paper bag, in a rolled up newspaper, and in a wallet, checkbook, purse, or briefcase.

An advantage is that these weapons will not show up on a magnetic weapons detector. When packed in a briefcase or other carry-on luggage, these glass fiber knives are practically invisible among other items under X-ray examination.

These are available from:

L.L. BASTON CO.
PO Box 1995-Dept. L
El Dorado, AR 71730

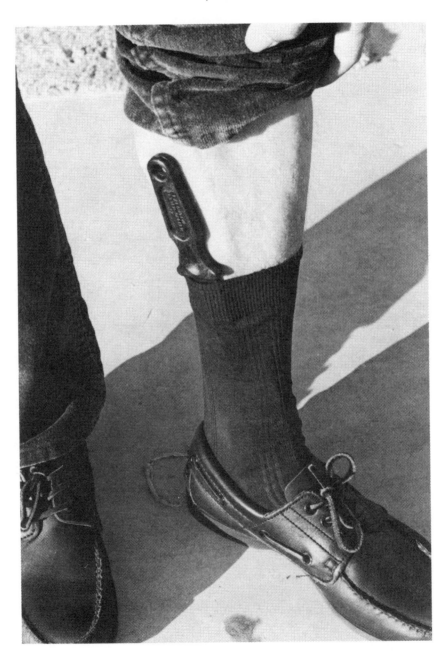

IMPACT WEAPONS

These can be anything, from a 2″ x 4″ to a piece of rebar wrapped with tape. Some can be relatively mild, such as a lead filled leather "sap," and others can be deadly. Impact weapons are easy to improvise and conceal.

One high class impact weapon that demands some skill is the Monadnock PR-16 collapsible side-handle baton. This is a 20th century outgrowth of the original Okinawan "tonfa." Many police officers carry the two-foot side-handle batons as standard equipment, because they've proven to be superior to the conventional police baton.

The PR-16 is a collapsible, 16-inch-long version, made of steel. Collapsed, it's only seven inches long, and the side handle is about five inches long. The whole affair fits in a leather belt holster collapsed, and drawing the weapon out with a snap opens it up in a threatening swing.

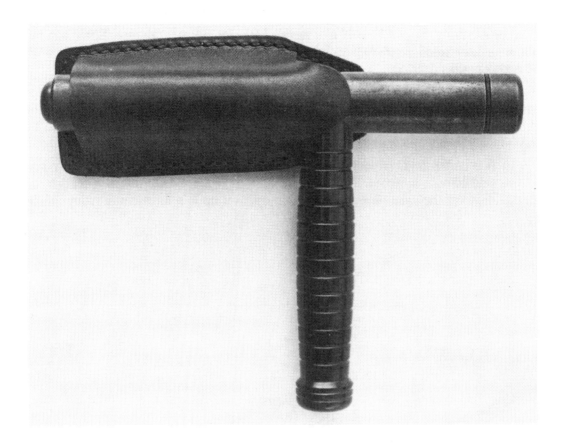

This device is obtainable from:

MONADNOCK LIFETIME PRODUCTS
PO Box B, Dept L
Fitzwilliam, NH 03447
Toll free 1-800-258-5492

GUNS

When we speak of a concealment weapon, or "hideout" gun, we mean a handgun. Handguns come in all types, but let's not make the mistake of thinking that only handguns are concealable personal weapons. Both rifles and shotguns are also concealable, because as we shall see, the amount of clothing you wear determines what you can conceal.

Revolver or auto? The auto pistol is slimmer than the revolver, and also shorter overall for the same or a similar caliber. Most auto pistols hold more shots than revolvers. Both can jam if not properly maintained and kept clean.

For most situations, a small or medium handgun will do. The calibers most commonly chosen for concealment use are .22 Long Rifle, .25ACP, .380 ACP, 9mm Luger, and .38 Special. In some situations, a .44 Special Charter Arms Bulldog is suitable, and some people even choose a semi-auto in caliber .45ACP. The .32ACP is not a common caliber on this side of the ocean.

A Sterling Model 302 is the minimum in guns. This is one of the most compact handguns you can find, with a two-inch barrel that doesn't quite use all of the power of the .22 cartridge. Truly, with this pistol, you sacrifice almost everything for compactness.

OTHER CONSIDERATIONS

What about "stopping power?" What about it? Unfortunately, even the experts disagree on exactly what "stopping power" is. Some rely on the old Hatcher formula, derived from some army tests of eight decades ago. Others have reworked the Hatcher formula without enhancing its already doubtful validity. The U.S. Department of Justice has published several projects, using modern ballistic data and computerized studies, but even these aren't immune to criticism.

The most important fact about firearms effectiveness is that you must hit where you're aiming. None of the other aspects are as vital as bullet placement. The ability to hit a fairly large target close up in poor light without using the sights, and under stress, is what makes the difference between life and death.

People who get shot go down faster than those who get knifed, but often not fast enough to please the frantic defender who may have only seen Hollywood or TV shootings. In films, shooting victims are thrown backwards, and they throw their guns out away from them as they fall. Those hit with shotguns seem always to get thrown through plate glass windows. In real life, reaction isn't that quick or spectacular, whatever the caliber used. The site of the hit is the important point.

Always keep in mind that the most important quality a defensive weapon must have is reliability. It absolutely must fire when you need it to. If you're going to keep a defensive weapon, test fire it with the ammunition you're going to use.

You also need something that you can fire accurately and comfortably. Does the gun fit your hand well? Is the recoil within your tolerance? Don't try to play "macho" and wear a gun that's too much for you. Seeing a big bore might frighten your opponent, but a solid hit with a smaller bore will put him down.

A couple of desirable features are a short barrel and small frame. For revolver fans, there are compact, lightweight versions of the duty rigs. The Smith Model 10 is available in four and two-inch barrel lengths. The Ruger Security Six comes in versions to please everybody: six, four, and two and three quarters inch barrels. Auto pistols also come in various barrel lengths. SIG makes a P226 service pistol with a double-column 15-round magazine, and the compact eight shot P225, with a single-column magazine, both in 9mm Luger. The shorter barrel usually involves a slight penalty in muzzle velocity, but this isn't as important as it may seem.

Bobbing the hammer of a revolver to prevent snagging on clothing during the draw is important. Some auto pistols also have hammers with long tangs, and are as likely to hook on clothing as revolvers.

CONCEALMENT ON THE PERSON

Let's start by stating the most important fact about concealing a weapon on the person. The most important determinant is the clothing worn. If you've got a car coat or an overcoat on, you can hide a carbine. If all you've got on is gym shorts, you'll be able to hide a much smaller weapon.

Climate determines the clothing. Local fashion also has something to do with it. In moderate weather, you're more likely to be able to wear a light topcoat in New York than in New Mexico. In some places, you stand out unless you dress like the natives. In a cold climate, you should be able to carry a full size pistol concealed. You can even hide a shotgun or carbine under a topcoat.

Generally, concealed carry is a compromise between concealment and quickness of draw. The more deeply buried the weapon is in the clothing, the longer it takes to bring it into play.

POCKET OR HOLSTER?

Americans favor holsters. Europeans still tend to use "pocket pistols" the way they were intended. Let's look at the advantages of both methods of carry.

A holster keeps the handgun in a secure place, instead of loose in the pocket. In a pocket, the handgun's likely to shift, and even to turn upside down. Its finish will suffer from contact with keys, coins, etc. A holstered handgun is more secure than one just tucked into the waistband. The pistol will eventually wear out the pocket.

Leather holsters tend to be expensive, although the new synthetic material holsters are reasonably priced. It's still cheaper to carry a gun in the pocket. Pocket carry's also more flexible. All you need to do is take it out of one pocket and put it in another. If you buy a holster, you're locked in. If it's an ankle holster, that's what it remains. There are some ambidextrous belt and shoulder holsters, though. Any holster adds some bulk. Another advantage of pocket carry is that in an emergency it's possible to fire the handgun from the pocket, although there's a risk of snagging the lining. Holsters usually don't permit this.

TYPES OF HOLSTERS

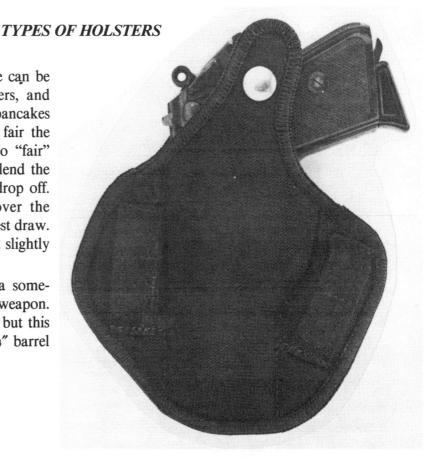

Let's start with belt holsters. These can be regular drop holsters, "slide" holsters, and "pancake" holsters. The slides and pancakes tend to place the pistol higher, and fair the contours of the gun to the body. To "fair" means to include extra material to blend the lines in, rather than having a sharp drop off. The holster can be at the front, over the appendix, which makes for the quickest draw. It's only necessary to open the jacket slightly to reach it.

The ERMA EXCAM RX-22 is a somewhat larger and much more effective weapon. Again, it uses the .22 caliber rimfire, but this one will develop 1250 fps out of its 3¼″ barrel when firing CCI Stingers. The "Gun Stuff" pancake holster is compact and convenient for carry at the waist. This one's available from:

GUN STUFF, Dept. L,

692 South Main

PO Box 1027

Moab, UT 84532.

The holster can be at the hip, which decreases the chance of someone seeing it if the jacket flaps open momentarily, but it's a somewhat slower draw. The worst position to carry, but perversely the most stylish, is the "FBI carry," over the kidney. The gun's most out of view, but drawing requires you to push the jacket all the way back and even lean forward. Another point: try to sit on a chair or car seat with one of these digging into your back. Worse, try to draw while seated. You need "elbow room," and even if you're only backed against a wall, you'll be impeded.

If you prefer a belt holster, and you need to draw it quickly, keep it forward over the appendix and keep your jacket buttoned. You can always rip the bottom off if you have to.

An extreme position is in the small of the back, over the spine. This usually means a tiny pistol tucked into your belt and perhaps held with a "Gun Clip," but it's fairly well concealed if you are fairly sure you won't need it in a hurry.

An unusual approach is this wallet-style holster, with an ASTRA "Cub" .25-caliber pistol. This permits carry in a back pocket.

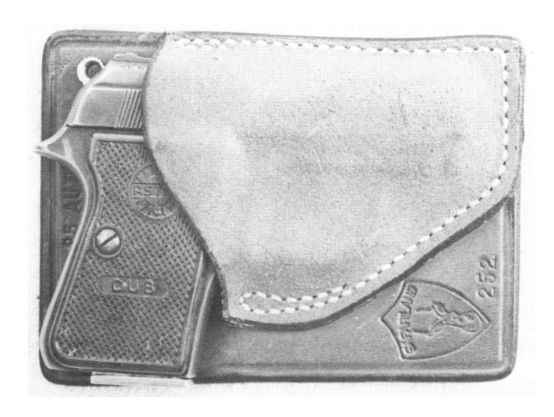

The smaller calibers are the popular choices because the handguns are small and easy to conceal, by both men and women, in light and medium clothing. An overcoat will allow carrying a sawed-off shotgun or a carbine.

The SIG P230 is an excellent compromise between power and size. This auto pistol's scarcely heavier than the ERMA EXCAM, yet it fires the .380 ACP cartridge. With Winchester Silvertips, the 85 grain bullets come out at over 1000 fps, enough to expand reliably. Mechanically, the P230 is one of the most reliable ones made. The source for the P230 is:

SIGARMS, Dept. L.
8330 Old Courthouse Road
Suite 885
Tysons Center, VA 22180

The Renegade "Ghost" holster is of a type known as a "maximum concealment" holster. It holds the small Smith & Wesson "Chief" revolver under the shirt, pants, and belt. It's slow on the draw, because you have to pull your shirt out of your pants to get at it, but will survive a quick pat down. The .38 Special round is adequate, even out of the short barrel. The "Ghost" came from Renegade Holster & Leather Company, which is now out of business.

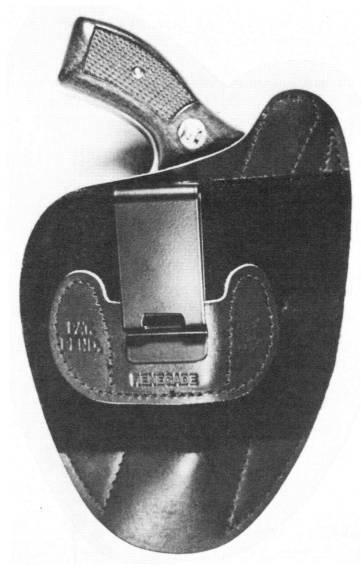

The "Badger" shoulder holster is the most concealable of the shoulder holsters made. This is because it provides fairing to mask the outline of the handgun. This hides even a bulky six shot revolver. The two points to watch are that the Badger must be adjusted to hold the pistol barrel up, and that the grip must not be too bulky. The Badger comes from:

SPECIAL WEAPONS, Dept. L

8740 Flower Road

Rancho Cucamonga, CA 91730

The shoulder holster's design is almost as old as the belt holster. This is a holster and harness to hold the pistol under the armpit. There are two types of shoulder holster, vertical and horizontal, and the terms refer to the position of the gun barrel. A vertical holster has the barrel pointing vertically, and the draw is up and out. Some models allow you to "rock" the pistol out, against a snap or a strap.

A larger pistol that lends itself to concealment is the very reliable 9mm SIG P226, a 15 round magazine model that fits well in a Galco Big Game Holster. The simple truth is that the main point about carrying a concealed weapon is the amount of clothing you're wearing. A heavy coat or jacket will conceal a surprisingly big weapon. For this class of weapon, the Big Game Holster is obtainable from:

GALCO INTERNATIONAL, Dept. L
4311 West Van Buren
Phoenix, AZ 85043

A point to watch, if you decide on a horizontal holster carry, is that the barrel should not be exactly horizontal, but angled slightly upward. This allows the butt to drop down, in keeping with the contours of the body. This aids concealment. It also allows you a somewhat quicker draw.

To give you an idea of what it's possible to conceal, this scope equipped Safari "Ultimate" pistol on a sling fits under a coat. To bring it into use, it's only necessary to unzip the coat and swing the weapon up.

It's possible to use accessories to conceal a weapon. A paper bag will do in a pinch, but a specially designed "Executive Protection Briefcase" is made to hold both a sheet of ballistic armor and a handgun in a special compartment.

To gain access to the revolver, you slip your hand inside the slot, prying the Velcro fastener apart. The briefcase comes from SPECIAL WEAPONS.

An ankle holster's another way to go. They're made both for small revolvers and for auto pistols, as is this SPECIAL WEAPONS rig. The Walther PPK fits adequately, but ankle holsters generally are slightly slow on the draw. One important point to watch is to keep the holster on the opposite inside ankle, so that a "bump frisk" won't reveal it.

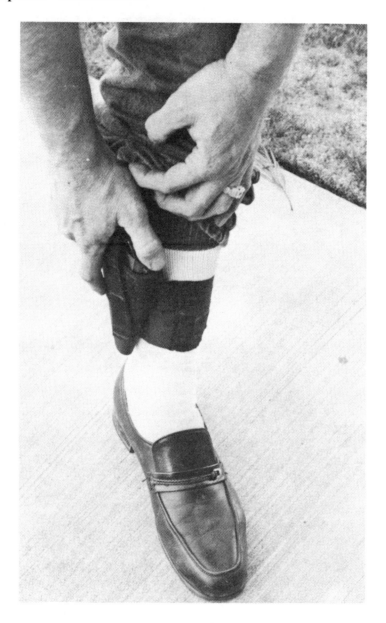

The ankle holster's been gaining in vogue. In warm climates, wearing a jacket can be very uncomfortable, ruling out shoulder or belt holsters. This holster is not quite as suited for absolute concealment as it is for "social" concealment. An ankle holster will not survive a search any better than most other holsters, but it allows plainclothes police to go about without displaying their guns openly. This is handy for administrative officers. The main tip off that someone's wearing an ankle holster is flared trouser cuffs.

One controversial point regarding ankle holsters is the question of a calf strap. Some users and some manufacturers swear by them. Others swear at them. It's largely a matter of personal preference, and comfort.

Drawing from an ankle holster is awkward. It's necessary to lift the cuff with one hand, to clear the gun for drawing with the other. You either bend down or lift your leg, and both are awkward in a gunfight. The ankle holster's really for the person who knows he won't have to draw in a hurry.

Another question relates to the security of the gun while running. If you anticipate having to run with a gun, check this out first. In this regard, you might find a thumbsnap more secure than a Velcro closure. A thumbsnap is either on or it isn't. A Velcro closure can be partly attached, especially if you fastened it in a hurry, and ready to break free under stress.

A final, low cost possibility is the "Gun Clip." This is a simple stainless steel belt clip and nylon lanyard which holds the handgun in the waistband and prevents it from dropping down the pants. It's reasonably secure, although not as much as a good holster, and it's very versatile. This comes from:

GUNCLIP, Dept. L
PO Box 740007
New Orleans, LA 70174-0007

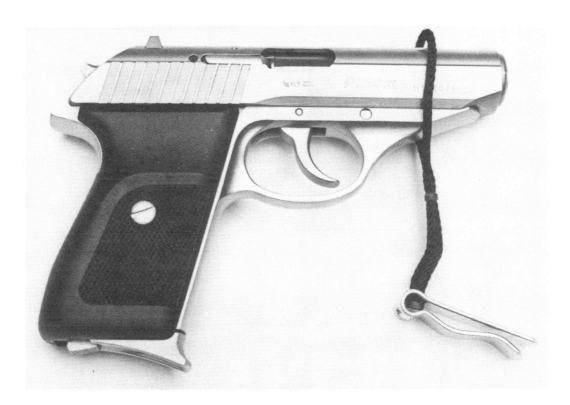

AMMUNITION

The question of what sort of ammunition to use offers an opportunity for another dissertation on "stopping power." Let's not waste time on that, however. Let's just note that the ammunition should be perfectly compatible with the gun, and not pose any problems in ignition, feeding, or extraction of fired cases. Reliability is the key.

With the smaller handguns, the question of hollow point ammunition becomes very troublesome. The short barrels simply don't allow enough velocity to develop for reliable expansion. A 110 grain hollow point load that comes out of a six inch barrel at over 1100 feet per second won't develop that from a two inch barrel. A more likely figure is somewhat over 900 feet per second and this is not quite the "threshold of expansion."

One notably good performer, if your taste runs to the .22 Long Rifle, is the CCI "Stinger." This round develops about 1250 feet per second out of the ERMA EXCAM RX-22 pistol, with a 3¼″ barrel. This is enough to cause the bullet to expand to about 45 caliber in water.

Although statistics from several sources tell us that the "average" gunfight is over within two or three rounds, not all shootouts are "average" and most of us feel more comfortable with a supply of spare ammo on hand. Some carry spare ammo in belt carriers or pouches. An awkward point is using speedloaders with revolvers. Although these handy devices enable a revolver shooter to reload much more quickly than possible without them, they're bulky, and for concealed use they're not as flat and concealable as auto pistol magazines.

"Loose change," carrying cartridges loose in the pocket, is a simple way of handling the problem of spare ammo. It's the slowest way to reload, but reloading probably won't be necessary. Carrying the ammo in a side pocket also helps if you have a belt holster. The weight of the cartridges keeps the jacket flap out of the way a fraction of a second longer when you flip it for the draw.

Speedloaders for revolvers are bulky. This makes them hard to conceal except under heavy clothing.

Auto pistol magazines typically are flat and compact. The double column ones are fatter, but not as bulky as speedloaders. This is a point in favor of auto pistols as concealment weapons.

A CONCEALED WEAPON MAY SAVE YOUR LIFE!

It's unfortunate, but true, that if you live in certain locales, or travel to certain places or by certain means, you will be in unreasonable danger. The authorities can't protect you all of the time. Unless you can afford a 24 hour corps of bodyguards, your safety's up to you. In some situations, you may feel it wise to carry a concealed weapon. If you do, remember that concealing it is only half the task. Using it proficiently and with good judgment's equally important. That's what the next chapter covers.

TACTICS FOR EMPLOYING
CONCEALED WEAPONS

There are several important points to note about using a concealed weapon in self-defense. The first is that you may be in conflict with the law merely carrying it, as we've seen. Another is that the legal aspect influences your actions afterwards. The illegally armed citizen who waits for the police will face prosecution. He'll also face crucifixion in the press, which will immediately label him a "vigilante." Finally, because robbers and muggers prefer not to have witnesses, the defender will most likely be alone with his assailants. This simplifies the problem of walking away from the situation after it's over. Many will be tempted to do so, to save themselves the hassle.

The word "vigilante" is so fashionable, and so common, that it's often misused. Anyone who uses force to save himself from becoming the victim of a crime is not a vigilante. The true vigilante is the one who, without being in danger or after the danger has passed, uses force against the alleged criminal. The press often confuse the two, although the distinction is very clear and simple. The vigilante undertakes the enforcement of the law. The defender is only protecting himself against immediate and serious danger.

MUGGERS

Although Hollywood rarely makes any truly true-to-life films, there's a significant exception, the film *Death Wish*. The realistic one is the first film, not the two sequels. In the original film, the script follows the novel quite closely, and the tactics used by Charles Bronson are realistic. In fact, he makes only two tactical errors in the whole film, both concerned with selection of which suspect to shoot first.

Let's go over the major tactical points. This will be useful not because you're going to go out in the streets and subways as a vigilante, but because the situation's the same, whatever your intent.

First, the defender uses the pistol one-handed. This is usually because the other hand's occupied with something else, or there's no time to bring the pistol up in a two-handed grip and take careful aim through the sights. The light's also bad, which impedes the use of the sights.

Secondly, note the speed at which events happen. Unlike most Hollywood gunfights the action's over in a few seconds. That's how long you've got to determine whether you're going to be reading about it in the next morning's paper, or whether your reading career's over.

Another point is: expect to get hurt. Only in cowboy and hero detective films do the good guys go through shattering gunfights without ever getting hit. In street and subway mugging, the bad guys are often so close that you can't be sure of stopping them, except with a rocket launcher or a flamethrower. There may be more than one, and if they're within five feet of you, you're unlikely to put both of them down before one of them gets you, no matter how powerful your weapon.

On this point, understand the need to keep your distance if the situation allows. If you can keep your attackers ten or more feet away from you, this gives you time to react and open fire when they launch their assault. Unfortunately, assailants try to take their victims by surprise, and often don't reveal their intentions until they're snuggled up close to their prey. It's remarkably easy to do in the city. Streets and subways are crowded. People press against each other, and often there's no warning at all.

The next major point is that the defender flees as soon as possible. In a shootout, you don't want to hang around giving explanations to the police, if you can avoid it. Let's face it, no matter how right you are, and how wrong the mugger is, the police aren't going to be giving you any medals. They'll treat you like a suspect. This is a disturbing, but real, aspect of the whole business.

Under American law, you're innocent until proven guilty. That's the law, but under police investigation, you'll be made to feel guilty, struggling to prove yourself innocent. You'll find detectives asking you to tell your account over and over, while looking at you with skeptical eyes.

Be realistic. Walk away after the shootout. Put the weapon back in your pocket, or holster, and leave by the quickest route. If you meet anyone running towards the scene, perhaps a police officer attracted by the gunfire, you can pretend to be a witness and say that the guy who did the shooting ran in the opposite direction. On a subway, immediately cross to the next car and leave the train at the next station. Let the bad guy ride to the end of the line.

In your home, you're not likely to be able to walk away from the scene. If an intrusion occurs, you may kill the suspect, or if the situation allows, you may capture him. If so, you may hold him at gunpoint for the police, or you may decide to search him to ensure your own safety.

SEARCHING A SUSPECT

You should be aware of places of concealment for weapons, in case you decide to capture and hold an assailant or intruder for the police. A concealed weapon might be as small as a single-edged razor blade, but it can be very troublesome if a suspect catches you off guard, and it can be lethal.

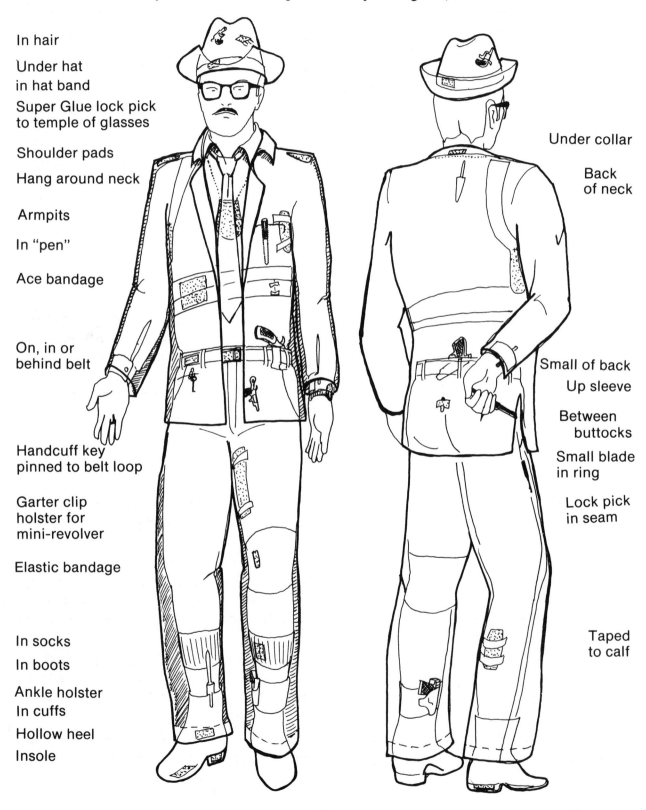

In hair

Under hat
in hat band

Super Glue lock pick
to temple of glasses

Shoulder pads

Hang around neck

Armpits

In "pen"

Ace bandage

On, in or
behind belt

Handcuff key
pinned to belt loop

Garter clip
holster for
mini-revolver

Elastic bandage

In socks

In boots

Ankle holster
In cuffs

Hollow heel

Insole

Under collar

Back
of neck

Small of back

Up sleeve

Between
buttocks

Small blade
in ring

Lock pick
in seam

Taped
to calf

The first step is to immobilize the suspect. Tell him to get down on the ground belly-down and to spread his arms and legs. Tell him to face away from you.

At this point, the safest course is to call the police or have someone do it, while you keep the suspect covered and threaten to shoot him if he moves. You might want to search him, though, for several reasons. One is a guard against becoming distracted. If he's got a weapon concealed, all it takes is a moment's inattention and he can hurt you. Another reason is that you might want him to get up to move to another room. If you permit him any movement at all, he might unmask a weapon. Yet another reason is if you turn over the task of guarding the suspect to someone else, while you attend to something more urgent. You wouldn't feel comfortable having your wife or other relative watching someone whom you hadn't rendered harmless to the limit of your ability.

Here's a quick rundown of some places where hoods can hide weapons: hair, headband, collar, down inside shirt, taped to the armpit, taped to the chest, at the belt, behind the belt, inside the waistband of the pants, inside the shorts, taped to the inside of the thigh, taped to the calf, inside the socks, inside the shoes, or tucked into a boot. Additional hiding places are between or under the breasts of a woman. A man may hide something small under the penis or foreskin, or behind the testicles. Both may hide something in the crack between the buttocks. However, these aren't usually hiding places for weapons, but for contraband, such as a small amount of drugs.

Searching involves feeling with a sliding motion, not a "pat down" as you see in the movies and on TV. A "pat down" can miss a lot. Sliding your hand is more likely to disclose something hidden under clothing. While feeling with one hand, keep the gun hand back close to your body, as far away from the suspect as possible.

Don't be shy when searching. A "streetwise" punk who has something hidden will try to fake you out. If he asks you, "Feel good, homo?" when you feel around his crotch, don't break off the search. He just might have something hidden right there. If you want to be thorough, do a strip search, in which he removes every article of clothing slowly, and tosses it away from him so that you can examine it. Doing the strip search this way avoids the danger of getting too close and giving him a chance for a surprise attack.

SPECIAL PROBLEMS

Some people take weapons with them wherever they go. This can be because they have a legitimate fear for their lives. There are some situations in which it's inadvisable, although possible, to take weapons.

One is on board aircraft. As we've seen, it's possible to smuggle even grenades on board aircraft. At least, terrorists know how to do it. Some civilians take glass fiber knives, which will pass through magnetic detectors and x-ray examination. A problem that comes up is that if a real skyjacking comes down on your flight, a knife may not be much help against a band of terrorists. Even if you managed to smuggle a firearm on board, the last thing you need is a shootout in the sky.

If you must travel from one locale to another and need to take weapons for use after arrival, it's usually possible to take them legally in your check in luggage. Airline people are usually very cooperative in this regard, and in some instances will even sell you a gun case at their cost so that you can check in firearms in compliance with federal regulations and airline procedures.

Airport security isn't all it should be, and if you're worried about being shot up in the terminal, your fear is realistic. It might happen. There are a couple of special points to note about your safety in a terminal.

The most important one is that certain airlines attract the attention of terrorists. Israel's El Al is the best known one. The lesson is clear. Don't travel on such airlines if you value your safety, and don't go near their offices or ticket counters. This isn't politics or anti-semitism. It's just a matter of saving your skin. After all, it's the only skin you have.

The second point is that if a shootout develops in the terminal, drawing a gun to defend yourself may also draw fire from the security troops. They're likely to shoot at anyone with a gun who is not one of the recognized security guards. You may easily be better off ducking for the floor and staying there until the smoke clears.

Keep an eye out for places of cover in a terminal. This is one way of passing the long, boring minutes before boarding. Another, very undramatic precaution is keeping a sharp eye on the other people. If you notice a group of people crowding together and fumbling with their luggage, watch them closely while you edge nearer to a corner and prepare to duck away.

THE BEST WEAPON

The best weapon you have is always away from view. It's between your ears, hidden in your cranial cavity. The best external weapon will result in your getting hurt if you don't use it prudently and proficiently. It's important to make the most of of what you have, and using your brain will help more than using your firepower.

SHIPPING WEAPONS CLANDESTINELY

The media image of the weapon smuggler is the terrorist, slipping his arms past national frontiers to harm women and children on the other side. This, like many of the fairy tales we are told by the media, is a distortion. In real life, there are some legitimate reasons for shipping weapons through without declaration and without detection. Most of these reasons are traceable to gun control laws.

Some people, in fear of their lives or carrying valuables, have good reason to travel armed, or at least to send weapons ahead so that they may pick them up when they arrive at their destinations. Some foreign countries, as well as some American jurisdictions, have firearms control laws so severe that the choice truly is either "tried by twelve or carried by six."

Within the United States, we have obstacles, local laws and the Gun Control Act of 1968. GCA 1968 prohibits interstate transportation or shipment of firearms except between federally licensed dealers. The penalties for violation include fines and prison sentences. Curiously, although this law was aimed at assassins, psychopaths, and terrorists when it was passed, the people against whom it's enforced are almost exclusively technical violators who commit infractions out of ignorance rather than during the commission of another crime. The reason is clear.

Agents of the Bureau of Alcohol, Tobacco, and Firearms find it easier to build up their arrest records by arresting technical violators. Assassins, terrorists, and other dangerous types would offer armed resistance to arrest, and cut short many promising careers in this branch of law enforcement.

One amazing, but little publicized, aspect of this is that a federal firearms license is incredibly easy to forge. It's a cheaply printed 5½" x 8½" piece of paper, and to make shipment of a firearm "legal" it's necessary only to send a photocopy of the original, not the original itself. The sender must sign the photocopy, according to the law, because a photocopied signature isn't valid. A hardened lawbreaker will find this bit of bureaucratic bumbling working to his advantage, because he can manufacture his paperwork so easily. He has only to use "white out" to cover the typed in name on a photocopy of someone else's license, and make a photocopy of that. He then types in his information, a license number, and he's set. Photocopying this "document" and signing each copy will allow him to have firearms shipped to him without undue delay.

However, a legitimate sportsman or hunter who travels from one state to another must be wary. The individual interested in self-protection must be even more careful, especially as he risks being labeled as a "vigilante."

Within this country, there are two easy ways to take or ship weapons without paperwork, with little risk, and with little delay. One is to take the weapon with you as check-in luggage. Federal rules require you to declare the weapon, but in practice few are ever caught at it. If you choose this course, make sure, absolutely sure, that the weapon is empty. It's illegal to ship a loaded weapon, period. But there's a more compelling reason. A few years ago an airline employee in Denver was killed when a weapon in someone's baggage discharged.

The other way is to ship by an air freight or express company. Such shipments are never x-rayed, because the sender has absolutely no control over when they become airborne, and by which aircraft. As we saw in the chapter on searchers, one airline, El Al, worries about the bomb in the luggage trick, and takes precautions with check-in as well as carry on baggage.

Shipping your weapon air freight or air express means that you'll be separated from it for awhile, but you can minimize this by having several, and shipping them ahead of you in your travels. Address them to "counter pick-up" so that you get access as soon as you arrive at your destination. That way, you'll always have one ready to pick up wherever you go.

If you have plenty of time, ship via ground transport. Nobody checks these packages, because nobody blows up trucks. Some people hijack trucks, but they don't hide inside boxes to do so.

Shipping to a foreign country can be problematic. The major obstacle is customs. It's practically always necessary to fill out a customs declaration and attach it to the package. Customs agents don't necessarily open every package for inspection, but often do impose a delay while they mull it over.

For shipment to a foreign country, the safest way is to conceal the weapon inside machinery. Customs agents will rarely tear apart a shipment of machinery far enough to uncover a weapon. The drawback is that this can impose quite a delay, because of the mode of transportation.

All considered, shipping weapons is sometimes a problem, but not one impossible to solve. The solution is often far less formidable than the law, and the reward can be substantial — having a weapon when you need it to save your life.